SECRETS OF

GREAT
RAINMAKERS

ALSO BY JEFFREY J. FOX

*How to Make Big Money in Your
Own Small Business*

*How to Become a Marketing
Superstar*

How to Become a Great Boss

Don't Send a CV

How to Become a Rainmaker

How to Become CEO

SECRETS OF

GREAT RAINMAKERS

The Keys to Success and Wealth

JEFFREY J. FOX

Vermilion
LONDON

3 5 7 9 10 8 6 4

First published in 2006 by Hyperion.
This edition published in 2006 by Vermilion,
an imprint of Ebury Publishing
Random House UK Ltd.
Random House, 20 Vauxhall Bridge Road
London SW1V 2SA

Addresses for companies within The Random House Group Limited
can be found at: www.randomhouse.co.uk/offices.htm

Random House UK Limited Reg. No. 954009
www.randomhouse.co.uk

Papers used by Vermilion are natural, recyclable products
made from wood grown in sustainable forests.

A CIP catalogue record is available for this book from
the British Library.

ISBN: 9780091954970

The Random House Group Limited supports The Forest Stewardship
Council® (FSC®), the leading international forest-certification organisation.
Our books carrying the FSC label are printed on FSC®-certified paper.
FSC is the only forest-certification scheme supported by the leading
environmental organisations, including Greenpeace. Our
paper procurement policy can be found at
www.randomhouse.co.uk/environment

MIX
Paper from
responsible sources
FSC® C016897

Printed and bound in Great Britain by Clays Ltd, St Ives plc

This book is dedicated to all the Rainmakers, paperboys, car washers, teachers, bartenders, oil changers, emissions inspectors, fitness trainers, rugby players, and moms and Nenas and Nannys and Grandma Kays and Gammys in the world.

CONTENTS

CONTENTS

CONTENTS

CONTENTS

{ x }

CONTENTS

{ **xi** }

CONTENTS

ACKNOWLEDGMENTS

Mary Ellen O'Neill, who, with the Hyperion team, got it done once again.

Doris Michaels of the DSM Literary Agency in NYC, who is a Rainmaker.

Heather and Damian Fox, who gave us Luca.

SECRETS OF

GREAT RAINMAKERS

INTRODUCTION

*I*t is easy to become an ordinary salesperson. The barriers to entry for a sales job are, in many companies, very low. In some companies the barriers to getting a sales job are so low a Galapagos turtle can jump over them. In some companies if you fog a mirror, you get the job. It is easy to become a salesperson. It is difficult to become a Rainmaker. Becoming a Rainmaker requires study, training, practice, and professionalism. A Rainmaker is professional in all things, small and big.

In companies that use salespeople to sell directly to customers, Rainmakers are the people who bring in the business. Rainmakers bring in big revenues, big money. Rainmakers bring in new revenues, new customers. Rainmakers sell new applications, new products, and price increases. Rainmakers make the cash register ring. Ka-ching! Ka-ching!

And Rainmakers make big money for themselves. Rainmakers are always the highest-paid sellers, and it is not uncommon for Rainmakers to be among the highest-paid employees in the organization.

Rainmakers are rare, but they are everywhere. They are in corporations as super sellers. They are commission-only salespeople, entrepreneurs, small business owners, solo practitioners, agents, brokers, partners in professional firms.

The difference between Rainmakers and ordinary salespeople is one thing: Rainmakers sell more! Rainmakers generate more sales revenues than the other people. They sell more through thick and thin. They sell more in good economies and bad. They sell more regardless of competition. They sell more regardless of price. They sell more despite internal company problems. Rainmakers sell more by relentlessly doing things that ordinary salespeople sometimes do or never do.

In a baseball game, a hitter or batter gets to the plate about four times a game. That means that the batter, barring a strikeout, and regardless of whether he gets a hit or not, has to run to first base three or four or five times a game. Even though running to first base three or four times a game is nothing, a small effort in the totality of the game, some players give up on their hit, assume they will make an out, and dog it to first. The Rainmaker never dogs it to first base! The Rainmaker never assumes he or she will be thrown out. The Rainmaker runs out every hit, and runs full tilt, because the few times the opposition fumbles the ball, or the ball drops in, the Rainmaker ends up safely on base. The Rainmaker never quits in the sales cycle. The Rainmaker always sprints, always goes for the sale. That's why Rainmakers are known as "big hitters."

This book contains the secrets of great Rainmakers. These secrets are why Rainmakers sell more and make more money than the rest of the selling crowd. Do what they do and go make rain!

• I •

A Career Odyssey: From Rookie to Rainmaker

*H*e was hired on a Friday. It was his first job out of college. On Monday he was selling. No sales training. Armed with product catalogues, brochures, and business cards, with scant direction, he was told to go down one side of the street and up the other, making cold calls. One day he made one hundred calls. Rejection, up to 90 percent and 100 percent on some days, was a brutal fact of his early selling career. At the time he did not know that cold calling is the least effective selling approach on the planet. Cold calling was what he was told to do. But all the rejection was a good thing.

He learned not to fear rejection. Rejection is a sales reality. Weirdly, he began to enjoy rejection. Each rejection was an opportunity for him to think on his feet, to experiment with responses, to toughen his resilience. Despite his sales manager's exhortations to "make more calls," he started to think. Cold selling was gambling. Rejection took many forms: The decision maker was out, in a meeting, too busy, sees people by appointment only, never heard of the salesperson, no solicitors allowed. He decided to improve the odds of making the sale. He focused on getting appointments via phone, note, visit. Thus, the next sales call was not a cold call. His hit rate soared and so did his career.

Early on, he decided he was not going to be serious about sales; he was going to be fiercely serious. He took every opportunity to associate with successful salespeople regardless of what they were selling. He schooled himself via books, audiotapes, and live professional sales training. Coincidentally, he read *How to Become a Rainmaker*. It is now his sales bible.

He wanted to become a Rainmaker from the top of his hat to the toe of his shoe.

The company assigned him to crack a big potential account that was dominated by another supplier. No one in his company had ever been invited to even make a proposal. He tried to penetrate the account according to his company's selling strategy. He stupidly repeated his company's prior experience. He was completely shut out. He considered handing the account to some other doomed soldier, but that was quitting. As with the cold-call situation, he started to think and to study. A complete review of the sales database and all sales call notes pointed out the obvious: He, and all the salespeople before him, had done the same thing. They called on the same contacts, wrote the same letters, asked the same questions. What they were doing failed, but they did not change their approach. He looked into the metaphorical mirror and asked, "What would a Rainmaker do?" Rainmakers are different from ordinary salespeople. They don't accept the rules for failure. Rainmakers adapt, change, take calculated risks. This Rainmaker, the guy in the mirror, decided to do everything new at the account, and to do nothing of the old. This Rainmaker was going to make rain. He formulated a new selling strategy. This decision would ultimately change his life, financially and professionally.

He knew he had to start selling to the top management of the customer. Everyone below top management had blown him off a number of times. Everyone says call on C-level, that is, CEO, COO, CFO, CIO. Easily said. He had never before called at the C-level. He was determined to do so whatever the risk of offending the lower-level people on whom he had been calling. Besides, he had no business with the company, so he had nothing to lose. He locked himself in his office and researched everything about the company, its industry, its competitors, its customers, its website. He learned that the real, but hidden, decision maker for the company was the chief financial officer. He tried to think like the CFO. But what did he know about running a multibillion-dollar, multinational company? He had trouble paying his own bills on time. Nevertheless, he put himself in the CFO's shoes. CFOs are interested in financial matters, especially in reducing costs. Based on his research, he concluded that his company could save the CFO's company at least $50,000 per year in reduced day-to-day operating costs. His plan was to phone the CFO and to get a sales call appointment. He carefully planned that phone call. He had learned the CFO's direct number. The CFO answered on the first ring. The salesperson introduced himself; said his call would be only a minute or two; told the CFO that he was confident he could save the CFO's company $50,000; and asked if the customer had his appointment calendar handy. The CFO did and they scheduled an appointment. The meeting with the CFO would be totally new and foreign, so the salesperson planned diligently. He brought one of his company's work-flow analysts with him to the meeting. Products were never mentioned on that first call because the salesperson's questions were focused on what the customer would gain from his products, not on the technology or features and benefits of the products. He offered to conduct a "cost savings discovery" to identify all unnecessary processes and other waste. Although the salesperson now charges to conduct a similar discovery, in this case he made the CFO an offer he could not refuse: The discovery would be free if no savings were found.

The CFO assigned a person in his company to work with the salesperson and to help get the information to correctly identify problems and solutions. Suddenly people who had previously ignored the salesperson, or said "no," were working with him. It was powerful leverage to have the CFO's backing, but the salesperson wanted to make the person assigned to him a hero, an ally, a champion. The salesperson gained his "champion's" trust when the ally realized the seller's only goals were to save the company money and to give the ally all the credit. The two people became friendly, and they hit a cost discovery home run. They showed the CFO a plan to save $5,000 a month (over and above the price of buying the products) in phase one of the cost-reduction project. This resulted in a $400,000 sale. The CFO approved phases two and three, which included additional investment in the seller's cost-reduction products throughout the United States and abroad. The CFO gave his approval after he reviewed the seller's detailed return-on-investment calculation.

Good things happen when you finally get in front of the ultimate decision maker. One of the reasons it took so long for the salesperson's company to crack this wonderful customer was that the traditional contacts said no because they could not say yes. The traditional contacts maintained existing relationships; they could not create new relationships. Don't take "no" from a person who cannot say "yes."

During the cost-reduction discovery process, the client ally casually mentioned that his son was a huge fan of the Oakland Raiders football team. Always listening, the Rainmaker mentally filed that fact. One week after receiving the first $400,000 order, the seller had personal plans to visit one of his best friends, who played for Oakland. Upon his return he gave his client ally a football signed by the Raiders, which he could give to his son. Remembering the little things and acting on them is never beneath a Rainmaker.

He made rain, money, for himself by making Rain—big money—for his customer. When the Rainmaker wins, the customer wins, and vice versa. This salesperson had raised his game to a new level, and went from rookie to Rainmaker.

Secrets of Great Rainmakers

• II •

Rainmakers Have No Competitors

Other salespeople and other companies want your customer. Other salespeople and other companies sell products and services like yours. Some of those products may have a lower price than yours. Some of those products may have different features or different technology or colors or sizes or delivery systems than yours. The other guys want your business. But they are not your competitors. Your only competition is customer ignorance.

If you believe in your dollarized selling proposition,

in the dollarized value your customer will get from your product benefits, and if you believe that if you were the customer you would buy from yourself, then you have no competitors. (Dollarization is the way to quantify—in dollars and cents—the true value of a product's benefits. For example, the dollarized value of less scrap could be $10,000 less in trash hauling fees.) Your only competition is that the customer does not yet know or believe in your dollarized value. The customer is ignorant as to why your solution is best. Your job is to educate the customer, to turn the customer's ignorance into understanding and into acceptance. Via careful questioning and listening, your job is to determine what the customer needs and knows and does not know. Your job is to uncover any customer mind-set or misconception. Your job is to ask questions that when answered help the customer to see your position. Apologizing for not having brought the customer new information—to help her decide—will enhance you in the eyes of the customer.

You can't control what the other guys are going to do. And the other guys are also honest, hardworking, and smart. But don't admit to having competitors. Never mention a so-called competitor by name. Never use the word "competition." Naming a competitor validates the competitor.

Never knock the competitor. Knocking a competitor insults your customer. Knocking the other guy or gal is tantamount to telling your customer that they are stupid for considering someone else. Knocking the customer will diminish you in the eyes of your customer.

Forget about the other guy. Stay close to your customer. Educate the customer. The other guy will have to react to you.

When you believe you have no competitor, it is totally in your control to make, or not make, the sale.

RAINMAKERS...

• III •

Rainmaker
Mottos

Mottos are rules to live by, to work by. Great
organizations have mottos. The Boy Scouts'
motto is "Be Prepared." The United States Coast
Guard motto is *"Semper Paratus"* ("always ready").
IBM's motto is "Think."

Rainmakers love mottos. Mottos remind Rainmakers what it takes to make rain. Some Rainmakers
have many mottos; some have one. Some have unartic-
ulated mottos. But probe a Rainmaker and you'll find a
motto, or mottos. Here are some Rainmaker mottos:

1. "EARLY TO BED, EARLY TO RISE, SELL HARD, AND DOLLARIZE."

Rainmakers sell "feel good," or money, or both. Rainmakers do not sell products or services. Rainmakers don't sell features or benefits. Rainmakers don't sell technology. Rainmakers sell what customers get from product benefits, or get from the technology. Rainmakers sell the dollarized value of product benefits and technology. When Rainmakers are selling a solution to a customer's problem, that solution is always dollarized, always expressed in dollars and cents. The Rainmaker always educates the customer as to how much money it will cost the customer to go without the solution.

Rainmakers take care of themselves. They work hard to sell hard. They are always in the selling game.

2. "IF YOU DON'T DO BUSINESS WITH ME, WE BOTH LOSE."

The Rainmaker absolutely believes, without a dollop of doubt, that he or she always improves the customer's current state. The Rainmaker knows that if the customer does not buy, then the customer loses something, and the Rainmaker loses the sale.

3. "I'M AWAKE, I'M WORKING."

Rainmakers are always in the game. Ordinary salespeople sell to live. Rainmakers live to sell. When the Rainmaker's alarm goes off at 5:00 A.M., it doesn't ring or play music, it sings out, "Hey, Rainmaker, it's selling time!" And the Rainmaker gets awake and gets selling. Any time, all the time, it's selling time.

4. "COMPETE FOR INCHES."

Like professional athletes, Rainmakers compete for inches. They make more calls, do more precall planning, and work harder than ordinary salespeople. They pay attention to all the little things. There are no typos in their letters. They don't wear ink pens in their shirt pockets. They are professional in every way. They know that an inch short is a lost sale.

5. "THE FUTURE IS NOW."

George Allen, Hall of Fame National Football League coach, had the same motto. That's why

Rainmakers first work to keep the business they have now. Rainmakers go for sales they can make this fiscal year. That's why they always try for a one-call close; ask for something, if not the order, on every call; don't rely on long-term relationships for today's sale. "Now" means now, today. Do something today. Don't procrastinate. Call a customer today. Right now.

• IV •

"You Can't Sell Beer Sitting at Your Desk"

Nemesio Diez Riega, a legendary sales manager at Groupo Modelo (the first-class, world-class brewer and seller of Corona Extra, Corona Light, and Modelo beer brands), exhorted his salespeople that sales are made on the street, face-to-face with customers. Unless you are a telemarketing salesperson, or a reactive order taker, the more time you spend in your office, the less money you will make. Given excellent precall planning and lead qualification, the more customers you talk to, the more sales you will make. There are a million reasons why it is tough to get in front of decision makers. And sitting at a desk doing busywork, procrastinating, hoping for the phone to ring, and kidding yourself is one of the million reasons.

Unless your customers come to you, you must go to them. Your office is airplane seat 3-C, or your car. Your desk is your briefcase. Your work day is all day. Your work week is all week.

When people are looking for a job, they are constantly networking, finding leads, following up on leads, sending letters, sending résumés, making phone calls, getting meetings and interviews. Selling is like looking for a job . . . every day. Selling is especially like getting a job if you are supposed to sell yourself to bring in new customers, sell new applications for existing products, sell new products to existing customers, open new markets, keep an important customer from leaving. Investing the same energy into selling as one does in getting a job is a high-return activity.

Sales calls on decision makers are rare. Salespeople who ask for a commitment from a customer are even rarer. (Studies show that 90 percent of all sales-people never ask for the order.) This means that the salesperson who gets meetings with customers, and who asks for the order, has a tremendous competi-tive advantage over other salespeople. Customers are more likely to say "yes" if asked than not asked. Cus-tomers are more likely to say "yes" if they are asked in a face-to-face meeting. That's why Rainmakers get out of their office and into their customer's office.

You can't sell beer sitting at a desk. You can't sell advertising, insurance, MRI machines, software sit-ting at a desk. You can't sell much of anything with-out meeting the customer.

"A lime with your Corona?"

Heed the First Buy Signal

Your appointment is at 10:15 A.M. You meet the customer on time. The customer opens the sales call by saying, "We are doing business with your competitor. Your competitor is a good company, their products are good, and their prices are cheaper than yours. That's it." The customer then folds his arms and leans back in his chair.

When this happens, if you do not understand what is really going on, and if you are unprepared, you might shrink and melt into a puddle of putty. But nota bene: The customer already knows he is doing business with a company he assumes is your competitor. The customer already knows his present supplier is a good company with good products. The customer already knows something about your products, and he knows your products have higher prices than what he is currently buying. So why did the customer agree to see you? He agreed to see you because he has a problem, and he thinks you might be able to solve it!

What the first-meeting customer is really saying is, "Look. I made a mistake hiring my present supplier. But I can't admit the mistake or it will hurt my career. I have a problem and I need a dramatic solution that I can bring to my company before this bites me in the butt. Please, please, please help me. But let me act like a tough guy, for a while, and let me save face. OK, now say something that will let me help you help me." That's what the customer is thinking.

Customer buy signals are acts in words or deeds that suggest a propensity to agree, to continue, to buy. Buy signals include customer smiles, nodding heads, agreements to test, technical questions, scheduling another meeting. But the first buy signal is when the customer agrees to see the salesperson, to make an appointment, to take the meeting. In today's busy world, decision makers do not schedule sales calls unless they have a need. Busy decision makers do not schedule sales call appointments because they are interested in what kind of clothes salespeople are wearing. Busy decision makers don't make frivolous meetings. If the customer agrees to meet, the customer has a need.

Because you have done exhaustive precall homework and research, and because you have painstakingly planned your meeting, you have a good idea as to why the customer should do business with you, and because you know why you would do business with yourself—if you were the customer—you have bedrock confidence in yourself, your company, your product. And because you know what the customer is really saying, you are calm.

You have your first buy signal; go for the sale.

You respond to the customer by saying, "Thank

you for taking some time to talk to me. Based on our experience with companies like yours, and based on my research, we are confident we can save your company at least thirty thousand dollars in reduced water usage. May I continue?"

Then you continue asking the forty or fifty questions you have thoughtfully prepared, written out, and practiced.

Turn the first buy signal into a buy.

• VI •

Turn Six into $60,000

The out-of-towner had a problem: He needed six
suspender (or braces) buttons installed on a pair
of expensive slacks that he planned to wear that eve-
ning. It was Parents' Weekend and he was visiting his
son, who was a freshman at a local private school.
The man was from Tennessee and was unfamiliar
with the town where his son went to school. First,
he stopped at a dry cleaner to see if he could get
someone to sew on the buttons. The dry cleaner sent
out clothes for repairs and could not help. Next he

went to a seamstress, who said she was too busy. She was making a customer a cocktail party dress.

Finally he went into a men's clothing store figuring the people might recommend a local tailor. Upon hearing the visitor's story and request, the retailer suggested, "We have a tailor on staff. He will be happy to sew on the buttons. It will save you some time. There will be no charge. And welcome to our pretty little town."

The visitor handed the retailer the trousers and the buttons. After a quick glance at the buttons, the clothier suggested, "May I make a recommendation on the buttons? My recommendation is that you substitute these handsome bone buttons for your buttons." The visitor answered, "Fine. How much will I owe you?" The retailer answered, "There is no charge. And keep your buttons for when your son wears suspenders." In a few minutes, the newly buttoned slacks were presented . . . wrapped and ribboned.

The next day, the man from Tennessee returned to the store with his wife and son. They spent three hours shopping for their son. They bought jackets and slacks and shirts and, of course, braces. That was the first sale to the visitor from Tennessee and it was a substantial sale. Over the next several years, the man from Tennessee, and his friends, and his son's friends, spent $60,000 in that clothing store.

Six buttons. Ten minutes. Uncommon courtesy. Accommodating attitude. Knowing that everyone is a potential customer. Little extras (the wrapping and ribbons) on top of extras (the bone buttons). That's all it took to turn six buttons into $60,000.

Wonder where the wife of the man from Tennessee gets her cocktail party dresses?

• VII •

Selling Is a
Contact Sport

Contact sports are hockey, football, soccer, la-crosse, boxing, wrestling, rugby, fencing, and more. In these sports players come into physical contact with each other, ergo, "contact sport." Contact sports are often rough. Other contact sports are baseball, golf, tennis, badminton, where keeping an eye on the ball is crucial for success. Good players are fearless, tough, physically fit. Good players practice constantly. Good players play to win and never quit.

Selling is a contact sport. Successful sellers are

constantly contacting new prospects via mail, phone, visits. Rainmakers are in constant contact with existing customers. Rainmakers know that face-to-face contact with decision makers is when sales are made.

Like other contact sports, selling is rough and tough. Customers can be brutal. Every other salesperson is fighting to get your customers and win the race to get new customers. Markets can decline, capacity can increase, prices can soften, technologies can change. Some salespeople think that gladiators (the ultimate contact sport) have an easier job.

Like great athletes, Rainmakers constantly practice, prepare, and plan meticulously, go to the plate, and swing the bat. And because selling is a contact sport, Rainmakers have fun; they are playing in a big game. They love the wins and forget the losses.

Contact a customer. Revisit an old contact. Ask people to suggest new contacts. Connect with the contacts. Close the sale.

Contact. Connect. Close.

Suit up. Enter the arena. Play the game. Play your sport.

· VIII ·

Play Rolodex Roulette

Your "people file" may be in a Rolodex, or on e-mail, or in an address book, or a rubber-banded pack of business cards. Wherever, however you keep your people file, you have to regularly use it, visit it, purge it, update it. Your people file has the names of customers, contacts, references, referrers, prospects, advisers, suppliers, friends, family. Your people file is full of people who can help you, and who are in continuous flux. Your people file is a boisterous mountain stream rolling gold nuggets by your fingers.

Every once in a while—at least once a month, or as often as the effort pays off—you must give your Rolodex a roll. Play Rolodex roulette. Give it a random roll and pick some names.

Put a chip on those names. Make a bet on those names. Think about those people. Call them. Talk to them. Listen to them. Let them know what's new with you and your company. Be sure they still know how you can help them. Be sure they know what you do to make a living. Be sure you are as up to date in their people file as they are in yours. Let them know how they can help you. Ask for something. Ask for a referral. Ask for a meeting. Ask them to call you sometime.

Keep your contact connections current. You are successful, or will be successful, and other people like to know and talk to successful people. Old contacts like to be called. They will be grateful. Some will feel remiss that they haven't called you. Your call removes a burden, restarts a relationship. Some may feel flattered. Few will be annoyed.

A bet on the Rolodex roulette wheel is the safest bet: It's a bet on yourself. Play Rolodex roulette and the chips will come your way.

Rainmaker roulette. Ka-ching! Ka-ching!

• IX •

How to Get an Appointment

*T*he sales process starts when you identify a target
customer. The process jump-starts when you
get a lead, an introduction, or a referral to the customer. With or without a lead the salesperson has to
find a way to get a face-to-face appointment with the
decision maker. Here is how Rainmakers get appointments with people they don't know:

1. Conduct extensive precall *homework* on target
accounts to identify decision makers; to identify

areas of need; to understand how the salesperson can help the customer; to get an idea of what it is costing the customer to go without the seller's services; to find a possible hot issue that is important to the decision maker.

2. After learning as much as possible, the Rainmaker moves from precall homework to precall *planning*. The Rainmaker maps out a blueprint to engage and sell the customer. The plan addresses potential customer concerns, the dollarized value of the seller's services, what questions to ask, what objections and barriers to overcome.

3. The sales plan includes crafting a three- or four-sentence letter to the decision maker. The objective of the letter is to get the customer to take a follow-up phone call from the salesperson. The letter does not try to sell the customer on anything other than taking the follow-up phone call. The letter presents a significant financial or personal benefit (or both) to the customer. This benefit must be so compelling that the customer is persuaded to take the phone call, or to call the salesperson after reading. Such letters should always include an intriguing postscript. Letter readers

always read postscripts. An example of a postscript that would interest a customer is: "I've talked to ten of your customers [or retailers or competitors or industry experts]. You'll be interested in what they are saying about you. I'll bring that information with me."

4. The letter is followed by a carefully preplanned and practiced phone call. The sole objective of the phone call is to get an appointment. The great salesperson does not try to sell anything during that phone call. The phone call is preplanned to handle two possibilities: (1) the customer actually answers the phone, or (2) you get voice mail. The phone call message reiterates the financial benefit(s) mentioned in the letter. If that message is accurate, relevant, and meaningful, the customer will be inclined to meet the salesperson. If that compelling message is left on voice mail, the customer will be inclined to get back to the salesperson or take the next call.

Here is an actual letter that got the customer decision maker to take the salesperson's call . . .

which led to an appointment, which resulted in a sale.

> Dear Hospital CEO [Use correctly spelled name]:
>
> Your hospital has 506 acute-care beds. Based on proven experience with other hospitals similar to yours, ABC Labs can save you at least $15,500 a year by eliminating redundant and unnecessary tests.
>
> It will take less than twenty minutes to show how you can recapture the $15,500. I will call you to schedule an appointment.
>
> > Medically yours,
> > Larry Labster
>
> P.S. There are seven other hospitals like yours that are now saving upward of $50K a year. I'll bring the case histories.

5. After the customer expresses interest in learning how the hospital can save $15,500, the Rainmaker

asks, "Do you have your appointment calendar handy?" Then the Rainmaker sets a date.

Do the precall homework. Do the precall planning. Write and send the letter. Make the phone call. Leave a message. Call back. Get an appointment. Make the sale. Make money.

• X •

How to Correctly Start Every Sales Call

There is archaic and misdirecting sales advice that recommends salespeople should start the sales call by trying to "bond" with the customer. This dumb advice suggests looking around the customer's office or workplace, spotting something, such as a stuffed walleyed pike, seizing upon the importance of the stuffed fish to the customer, and then asking, "So, I see you are a fisherman. Where did you catch that beauty?" As if the sales rep really cares!

The correct and professional way to start a sales

call is to ask, "Mr. Customer, I just want to confirm your time availability for this meeting. We agreed on the phone that this meeting would take about twenty minutes. Is that still OK with you?"

Asking this question does the following:

1. It confirms the time. The customer might say, "Sorry, I only have five minutes." (This answer means you must get to the point immediately. Present your dollarized benefit, and ask for the order. You will be ready to do this because you will have precall planned for this eventuality.)
2. If the customer says "yes" to the time frame, then the salesperson has gotten the all-important first "yes" in the sales cycle.
3. The customer is immediately engaged.
4. The question eliminates the common sales call agenda blocker: "How long is this guy going to take?"
5. The customer believes he or she is in control of the sales call.

6. The question presupposes that the salesperson made an appointment, and gave the customer the purpose for the meeting. That the customer agreed to see the salesperson is a buy signal. Saying "yes" reinforces the customer's positive attitude toward the seller's proposition.

Getting the customer to say "yes," to agree to the first step in the sale, is infinitely better than finding out on which golf course the customer shot his hole-in-one or in what dangerous jungle he bagged that monster chipmunk. After you get the order, and only if you care about the answer, you can ask a non-business question.

• XI •

The Real Secret About Asking for the Order

*A*sking for the order, the first rule of selling, must be a secret. Or, the act of asking for the order must be a dark, open secret, as so few salespeople ever ask. It is estimated that 90 percent of all salespeople never ask for the order. One open secret to the Rainmaker's success is that Rainmakers always ask for the order, or they ask for a customer commitment to an action that leads to an order. Every salesperson and sales manager and sales trainer knows that a salesperson is supposed to ask for the order, unless, of course, the customer steals the show, leaps from his chair, and screams, "Wrap it up. I'll take it. I'll buy it. I'm in. Here's the money; keep the change!" Every salesperson knows the "ask for the order" secret to successful selling, but maybe 10 percent of all salespeople actually ask.

Ordinary salespeople don't ask for the order because they fear rejection, don't know how to ask, don't believe they should ask, don't believe in their product, don't believe in their price. Ordinary salespeople don't ask for the order because they do not understand the customer's role in the buying process.

The real secret about asking for the order, the secret that fuels the Rainmaker's success, is that Rainmakers understand that the customer expects and wants the salesperson to ask questions, including asking for the customer's business. The Rainmaker knows that not asking for the order leaves the qualified customer uneasy, uncertain, dissatisfied. The customer who invests his or her time in a meeting with a salesperson does not want to waste that time. If a salesperson does not ask for some kind of commitment, the customer is thinking, "What was this guy doing here?" "Doesn't he value me as a customer?" "If the product is so good, how come he didn't ask me to at least try it?"

An internationally known charity, and a wonderful first-class, world-class organization, was concerned about the low percentage of meetings with prospective donors that resulted in charitable gifts. The charity's fund-raisers believed that when they first met with a prospective donor, the best gift-getting strategy was to "build a relationship" with the donor. The fund-raisers believed that a solid, personal relationship would eventually lead to a gift. Consequently, in the first meeting (and often in the second, third, and fourth meetings), the fund-raiser would spend the entire sales call "getting to know each other."

After such a meeting, the fund-raisers felt that everything went well. The donor served tea and cookies; they talked about gardens and grandchildren; everyone was giggles and smiles. The prospective donors thought differently. They wondered if they were the kind of people the charity desired. They wondered if the charity thought they could not or would not be able to cough up a proper donation. The prospective donors were unsettled, uncertain, not satisfied. The fund-raisers' "building relationships" strategy was really a socially acceptable excuse not to ask for the order, to avoid rejection. It was a selling approach that, to be successful, depended on the prospective donor taking action unilaterally, reaching out, grabbing the fund-raiser, and jamming a check into the fund-raiser's hand.

What the fund-raisers came to learn was that when a prospective donor agreed to a meeting, that agreement was a customer buy signal. The donors knew it was a charity calling. People know charities ask for money. So when the donor agreed to meet with a fund-raiser, the donor already knew the meeting was about donating.

When the fund-raisers understood the donor's (customer's) point of view, the selling approach changed. Now the fund-raiser, early in the call, asks the donor, "Mrs. Ross, Worldwide Charity depends on people like you to help fulfill its mission of helping the desperately poor. There are many ways you can help the poor. For example, it costs twenty-three dollars a night to feed and shelter a family of four. Some people donate money to help poor families for ten nights . . . or for a thousand nights. Other people look to help in other ways. May I explore some ideas with you?" With this more up-front approach, donations per fund-raising call are up 20 percent.

It is OK to ask for the order. Good customers expect and want you to ask for the order. Therefore, always, always, always ask for something. On your next sales call, why not try asking for the order? You might make rain.

• XII •

Take a Stroll

Rainmakers love customer tours. A factory tour is a great way to learn about the customer, to discover sales opportunities. A customer-led tour is a buy signal: The customer has elevated you from sales-rep status to guest status. Good customers love their companies and are proud of the place where they work, be it castle, garage, loft, an overturned Chevy under a bridge. Customers love to show interested people around. When customers become hosts, Rainmakers go on high receive. Customers relax,

{ 47 }

they're at home. They answer questions with candor. Anything the customer says, no matter how seemingly trivial, might be an important clue to making the sale.

In the sales process, the Rainmaker always asks for something. When the customer says "yes," the Rainmaker has a commitment to an action that leads to a sale. Thus, the Rainmaker always asks to take a stroll through the hot, oily, sweaty metal-cutting factory in the middle of August.

The customer was a big-city newspaper. The product was a $150,000 security system. The appointment was scheduled from 3:00 to 4:00 P.M. The salesperson felt that one hour would be barely enough time to present all the slides, show all the options, demonstrate the cameras. Walking into the meeting room, the salesperson instantly recognized that the group of customer decision makers looked beat, tired, no energy. After introductions, one of the customers said the group had planned to go to the company cafeteria much earlier, but the previous presentations ran over. Would the security system sales rep like to join them for a snack, a cup of coffee, a soda? The salesperson agreed to join, of course, but internally seethed that the shortened selling time would be fatal to her sale. During the stroll to the cafeteria, by asking questions the sales rep learned that three other security companies had pitched their wares that day. The rep learned that the customers' fatigue was a function of sitting quietly and passively through slides, slides, slides; drone, drone, drone; talk, talk, talk. One of the customers wearily asked how long the rep's presentation was. Instinctively, the salesperson changed her sales call strategy. Instead of talking and telling, as did the other vendors, the sales rep said, "Why don't you guys tell me what you want? Why don't you show me the areas where you need security and surveillance? Why don't we forget that little conference room and continue the stroll? Would you folks give me the grand tour and show me how you publish a newspaper?"

Magically, the energy was back. The newspaper people happily conducted the tour. They were proud of their newspaper. They explained the newspaper's history. They pointed out framed front-page scoops.

They showed their Pulitzer Prizes and other awards. At every stop and at every display, the sales rep asked questions, listened, and took notes. One of the customers mentioned that his car had been vandalized in the employee garage . . . was it possible to install some kind of security system in the garage?

The sales rep instantly stopped strolling and said to her hosts, "Yes, you can monitor the garage, and you can monitor the rest of your facility. You can get zoom-lens cameras that can see into every nook and cranny of the garage. You can get a security system that the bad guys will know is watching them. Vandalism and thefts will drop like a stone. And anybody stupid enough to break in will end up in jail. And you can make your great newspaper safe and secure starting tomorrow at 8:00 A.M. Will you let me secure your newspaper?" And then she waited. A $150,000 sale was in play. The only sound she could hear was the roar of her heart pounding in her ears. The newspaper people, the customers, looked at each other, gave each other the "why not" look. The man whose car was vandalized said, "Today, all day long, the other salespeople talked about themselves, showed slides of their stuff, pushed their agenda. You let us talk about us. It is the end of the day, and you are the only salesperson who knows what we need. If your zoom lens does what you say it does, then you've got the order." The sales rep thanked her hosts, scheduled the proper demonstrations, and left the building.

Part of precall planning is to plan to be flexible. Be ready to change tactics. Look for clues that suggest a change in tactics. Selling is not a walk in the park, but if you have to take a stroll, do so.

When offered, always take the tour, take the stroll. If not offered, always ask to take a tour. When the customer opens that door and politely waves you in, accept that invitation to sell.

• XIII •

The Fisherman

*T*he salesman sold tax shelters and financial products to high net worth individuals. He targeted doctors as his primary market. His products were well-suited to the needs and circumstances of doctors. His biggest problem was finding prospects and getting appointments. High compensation doctors worked long hours and had little time for anything, let alone salespeople. But the salesman knew that his products would make doctors money, and he knew the amount of money the doctors would make would be persuasive.

The salesman remembered one Rainmaker rule: "Fish where the big fish are." And then, eureka! The idea hit him. Hospitals! Clinics! Hospitals are full of doctors.

The salesman found the fish, but the fish were still too busy to bite. What to do? And then, eureka! (The salesman was big into the Greek word "eureka," which means "I found it.") The idea hit him. He would become fish bait. He booked himself for a complete physical at a world-famous clinic.

During the physical he met several physicians. He met a cardiologist and a urologist and an orthopedist and a proctologist. And with every doctor, the tax shelter salesman found an innocuous way to talk about the fabulous financial benefits offered by his products. He made lots of appointments, lots of sales, and got lots of referrals and introductions to see other doctors.

After his physical at the famous clinic, the salesman scheduled himself for complete physicals at a number of other large clinics and hospitals across the country. Henceforth, he visited only ponds full of big fish.

The financial products salesman met and sold neurologists, allergists, oncologists. He never felt better.

• XIV •

Why Customers Want
to Give Referrals

*A*ll the books on selling advise salespeople to ask their customers for referrals. A referral is the name of someone who could be a new customer. This advice is correct. Rainmakers always ask for referrals, but they ask using "aided prompts." Rainmakers help their customers to think of possible referrals with aided prompts: "Are there members of your country club . . . others in your family . . . people with whom you work . . . other softball players who might want to get the same deal you received?"

The reason why Rainmakers always ask for referrals and why ordinary salespeople rarely ask (despite the avalanche of advice) is that Rainmakers understand that *many customers want to be asked*. Rainmakers understand the psychology that stimulates referrers to refer.

Many buyers want reinforcement that they made the correct purchase decision. They want validation that they bought the right product; that they paid a good price, got the best deal, are in style, will get their money's worth, won't be disappointed. Giving the salesperson a referral is giving approval to the salesperson for selling. Giving a referral makes the referrer an authority on the salesperson's product. Giving a referral is a type of "word-of-mouth" advertising, the most powerful advertising medium on the planet.

Consider the customer who, unprompted, tells a friend that she discovered the coolest little handbag boutique, and had bought a one-of-a-kind handbag. Many customers like to be the discoverer. And when her friend visits the handbag boutique, the customer's purchase is validated. Consider the customer who "found" the newest Tuscan restaurant; or who moved her portfolio to a new stockbroker; or who has the sharpest divorce or tax attorney in town; or who knows the best place in Amsterdam to buy tulip bulbs. If this customer were asked for new customer referrals by the handbag retailer, the Tuscan restaurateur, the divorce or tax attorney, what would be her response? She would give some names of friends. To decline she must discredit her own discoveries and, thereby, discredit her decision-making ability. Most new, satisfied customers are loath to criticize themselves. Most happy customers are happy to help their salespeople make other people happy.

Rainmakers know a secret: Every sale starts with a lead, an introduction, a referral. Rainmakers know another secret: 75 percent, or more, of referrals from good customers become new customers. And those new customers lead to more new customers. Referrals make salespeople and customers happy.

Be happy!

"Get the Blank Out of Here"

*H*e sold for a respected hand tool company. He sold to owners of independent hardware stores. He was apace to win "Salesperson of the Year." He was young, but experienced, motivated, ambitious. His excellent products sold well at premium prices, generating significant revenues and gross profits for hardware stores. He carefully pre-planned every sales call, calculating in advance how much money his products would make for the hardware store owner. He viewed selling as a game of enrichment——enrichment for himself and for his customers——and not as adversarial or confrontational.

It was his first time in the account, so he asked a clerk to point out the storeowner. He walked past shoppers, approached the owner, and introduced himself: "Hi, I'm with Terrific Tools company." The owner looked at the young tool salesperson, turned radish-red, and, in front of the customers and clerks, thrust his hand toward the door and screamed, yelled, bellowed, "GET THE BLANK OUT OF HERE!"

The salesman felt the stares of the customers, and heard the silence as everyone stopped, mouths agape. The salesman clenched his briefcase. The salesman mentally smiled. The salesman did not take the red-faced scream personally, as he had never met the owner. The salesman thought to himself, "This guy is going to buy more tools today than he has ever bought in his life." The salesman said nothing and watched as the owner's outstretched arm slowly descended to the counter. When the owner regained his composure, the polite salesman asked, "Did Terrific Tools upset you somehow?" The owner vented that the previous Terrific Tools salesperson had mishandled his last order, undercredited the owner for returned tools, and been rude in the process. The tool salesman listened without interrupting. He nodded, took notes. The store owner went on and on. When the store owner was finished criticizing Terrific Tools, the salesman calmly said, "Well, that is probably why Terrific Tools assigned your account to me. I am here today to show you how you can make two thousand, four hundred and sixty dollars in additional sales revenues. May I take a few minutes and show you how you can get that two thousand, four hundred and sixty dollars?" For the next few minutes the salesman showed the owner how certain tool displays had an 80 percent probability of selling all the tools in four months. Thus, a $3,000 investment in displayed tools would result in retail sales of $5,460. The young salesman booked an order for $3,000. This order was the largest tool order the owner had ever made. But the owner would also make more money on that investment than he had ever made before.

After the sale, the young salesman headed to the door and got the blank out of there.

• XVI •

Something for Free Is Not a Loss Leader

A "loss leader" is when you sell a product or service below cost, in the forlorn hope the customer will buy something else, giving the seller a profit. Loss leaders lead to losing money. Loss leaders are losers. Lose the loss leader from your selling strategy. However, doing something, or giving the customer something for free, is not a loss leader. Something for free is a good customer getter.

A free sample is not a loss leader. If the customer will actually test the sample or try the sample or taste the sample, then the sample increases the chance to make the sale. (If the customer will not test the sample, then don't give a sample.) The delicatessen that displays a dish filled with free samples of cheese sells more cheese than the store that does not provide samples. A free drink with dinner sells more dinners. A free car wash upgrade sells more car washes. A free blood pressure test brings more customers in to the pharmacy. A free tour of a winery sells more wines. A free legal consultation generates more law firm clients.

Good customers understand what "free" means. Good customers know you are in business and that you can't afford to lose money. Good customers know that if they accept a sample, or agree to test a product, there is some good-faith understanding that a successful experience leads to a purchase.

A piece of bubble gum and a piece of paperboard are different products with different purchase motivations. Kids can buy bubble gum; they can buy sports cards; they can buy either separately. So why do kids buy millions of packs of sports cards, with each pack containing a piece of bubble gum? Do the kids buy the cards or the gum? The cards are collected, kept, or traded, so they have "life." The gum is chewed, savored, bubbled, and tossed. Kids are buying the cards, but the "free" bubble gum sells lots of cards.

Giving something away, giving the customer something for free, need not lose money. Free may incite a shopping spree.

• XVII •
Killer Sales Questions
#1 and #2

Rainmakers know that sales calls must always be made on decision makers. Unlike ordinary salespeople, Rainmakers don't waste selling time calling on people who are not decision makers or who are not important decision influencers. (Most salespeople fear rejection, fear hearing "no," and consciously or subconsciously, call on non–decision makers, because non–decision makers rarely say "no.") Rainmakers also know that there are always hidden decision makers. The number of hidden decision makers and in-

{ 64 }

fluencers increases as the amount of money increases, as the risk increases, as the potential change increases. This is particularly true in business-to-business sales. A good Rainmaker rule of thumb is to assume that there are ten to fifteen decision makers involved in most decisions. One crucial element to successful selling is determining who the decision makers are, and learning their objections or concerns about the purchase.

Rainmakers never assume the person with whom they are talking is the decision maker, or is the sole decision maker. Rainmakers always assume there are other decision makers. But finding the decision makers is not always easy. Sometimes a customer contact will claim to be the decision maker when he or she is not. This misdirection can be deliberate, to shield the true decision makers, or to impress the salesperson with the importance of the customer contact. Sometimes the contact will incorrectly think he or she is the decision maker. Sometimes a contact will say that he or she is not the decision maker when they are. Given this dilemma, salespeople are traditionally taught to ask their contact this question: "Are you the decision maker?" This question is improper. It puts the contact on the spot. The question can diminish the customer, or embarrass or cause the customer to fib.

Instead, Rainmakers always ask their contact this killer sales question, "*In addition to yourself,* who else is involved in making this solution happen in your company?" This question does not impugn, embarrass, or disparage the customer: It simply assumes reality.

After the customer fully answers the question, giving names, titles, responsibilities, the Rainmaker asks the second killer question: "And what might their concerns be about going ahead?" The answer to the second question blueprints the continuing selling strategy, the needs to address, the objections to handle, the customer consensus to get.

The answers to these two killer sales questions are the Rainmaker's roadmap.

• XVIII •

Always Get Your Customer
to Do Something

Customer participation leads to customer persuasion. Customers who taste a piece of prosciutto are more likely to buy prosciutto. Customers who take the offered pen are more likely to sign. Customers who use a calculator to understand the dollarized value they are getting are selling themselves. Customers who answer questions are participating. Customers who do research to find the best new resort are more likely to visit that resort than are people who learn about the resort in, say, an ad. The customer who tries or tests a product is more likely to buy the product than someone who simply takes a sample. A customer who pays for a sample is ten times more likely to test, try, and buy a product than a customer who pockets a free sample. Direct mail sellers of magazines have found that mailings that require customers to make an extra effort to affix stamps (representing magazine covers) to an order form get greater returns and sales of magazines than mailings in which customers order by simply checking boxes.

When your customer invests any effort, time, or money into the buying process, the customer is closer to buying than the noninvested customer. Therefore, always ask your customer to

- put down a deposit
- fill out a survey
- visit a website
- take a plant tour
- visit your place of business
- talk to references
- answer a question
- give their opinion

Let customer fill in the $500 amount on the form in the blank space.

{ 68 }

When the Rainmaker politely suggests to the customer, "Please sit here," and the customer sits there, a successful sales cycle has started.

Don't burden your customer. Don't make it hard for your customer. Don't put things on your customer's "to-do list." Do help your customer. Let your customer help you to help them.

When your customer does something at your request, the customer has made a concrete or tacit commitment. Commitments lead to a sale.

• XIX •

Paperboys

*A*uthor's note: In my book *How to Make Big Money in Your Own Small Business*, Chapter 12 is titled "Hire Ex-Paperboys." There are numerous reasons to hire ex-paperboys and papergirls. One reason is that successful paperboys are good salespeople. I don't know if in today's world being a paperboy is still a job option for kids, but it is astounding how many great bosses and how many Rainmakers were once paperboys. It is also remarkable how many paperboys appreciate how positive and formative that job was. An uncommonly high statistical percentage of the Rainmakers who contributed to this book are ex-paperboys.

He was ten years old (or twelve, or thirteen, or sixteen), wanted a motocross bike (or skis, or a model train, or a guitar, or whatever), but did not have the money. If he wanted the bike, he had to earn the money to pay for it. So he got a morning delivery paper route. The newspaper company would "sell" him fifty papers a day for 35 cents a paper, which he would resell to his customers for 40 cents a paper. (This paperboy grossed 5 cents a paper per day plus any tips.) Like all paperboys, he was responsible for forecasting how many papers he would sell, and then need to buy. He was responsible for selling the papers, delivering the papers, collecting the money, paying back the newspaper company. He was an entrepreneur, a businessman, a Rainmaker.

One early morning a customer met the paperboy on the driveway. The customer asked the paperboy if he wouldn't mind leaving the paper on the back porch as the customer was traveling and didn't want to announce his absence with the newspapers littering the front yard. And, the customer asked, would the paperboy wrap the papers in plastic to keep them dry? The kid did so willingly. The next week when the paperboy was collecting the week's money, the traveling customer gave him a generous tip. That generous tip was a big lesson for the paperboy. Wrapping papers might mean he could make more money, and making more money meant he could get that motocross bike sooner. The paperboy proceeded to interview every one of his seventy-eight other customers, asked if they had any delivery preferences, wanted bad weather wrapping, anything. Many did have a special request. The ten-year-old paperboy jokingly suggested "put me on your Christmas list if I deliver as promised."

The ten-year-old paperboy did what 90 percent of all ordinary salespeople never do, and what 100 percent of all Rainmakers always do: He asked for the order! And he got the order. Over half the customers on his route gave him generous Christmas and holiday tips. The kid saved enough money to buy the motocross bike.

Paperboys learn you can make it rain, and make

money when it's raining. You can make it rain when the sun shines. You can make it rain in the dark. You can make rain when attacked by wild beasts or ice-cubed by winter. You can make rain when everyone else is sleeping. You can make rain by wrapping the papers, delivering the papers on time, and collecting the money for papers delivered.

By listening to one customers needs he found a whole new way to add value.

• XX •

The Price Was Right

*I*t is OK to price your product for what it is worth. If your product or service provides more value than a similar product, you can charge a higher price. Too many salespeople cut their price at the slightest pressure from a customer. Too many salespeople don't truly believe in their price. Good customers don't mind paying a fair price to get the extra value. Customers that don't value your value are not worth the pursuit. If your product is priced to fairly reflect the value, stick with your price.

A customer walked into an upscale paint and wallpaper store. The store specialized in expert decorating advice. This valuable hard-to-get expertise was reflected in the small price premium the store charged for its products. The customer approached a young clerk and said, "This is the last weekend before the winter weather that I can stain my decks. How much is a gallon of Weather Wear porch and deck stain?" The young clerk told the customer it was $11.99 per gallon. The customer exclaimed, "Eleven ninety-nine per gallon?! I can get it down the street at ABC Store for nine ninety-nine." The clerk said, "Depending on how many gallons you need, and if you already know the best way to apply the stain, you might be better off getting the deck stain from those people." The customer said, "But ABC Store doesn't have any Weather Wear." The young clerk answered, "Well, when we don't have any Weather Wear, our price is also nine ninety-nine."

Product availability, product expertise, product pride is worth the additional $2.00.

When you price it right, the price is right.

Huge lesson.

Reductio Ad Absurdum

*E*very salesperson has experienced, or will experience, the "difficult" customer. This is the customer who makes outrageous demands, unreasonable requests. This is the customer whose wishes are so unrealistic, they border on the absurd. Often such requests are in the areas of pricing, extended payment terms, product return policies, delivery dates. The salesperson's job is to help the customer understand that what the customer is asking does not make sense, is impossible to provide, or might have negative consequences for the customer.

For example, the automobile manufacturer that dictates that its parts suppliers reduce their selling price 5 percent (or 3 percent or some percentage) per year, every year, does not understand that such a request is mathematically impossible. Reducing product prices by 5 percent per year means the price will ultimately reach zero. Long before the 5 percent price cutting erases profits, the parts suppliers will cut quality, cut service, or stop making the part.

A dump truck manufacturer was experiencing significant warranty costs because a transmission gasket occasionally leaked. The dump truck company was paying 92 cents for the leaking gasket. The company's purchasing people were talking to a new gasket supplier, whose gasket did not leak but was priced at $1.02. The purchasing agent said he would not pay 10 cents more, as he bought hundreds of thousands of the gaskets and did not want the huge increase in expenditures. The gasket salesperson suggested that if the purchasing agent were concerned about saving 10 cents, why not save the entire 92 cents and not put any gaskets into the transmission? The purchasing agent suggested, in turn, that the salesperson was crazy: not putting in gaskets would cause leaks. The salesperson asked, "So what if the transmissions leak?" Convinced the salesperson was deranged, the exasperated purchasing agent answered, "Because if the transmissions leak, we'll have unacceptable warranty claims, lose customers, lose money." The gasket salesperson immediately showed the customer that if 100 percent leaking transmissions were unacceptable, so too were 3 percent. The salesperson and the customer agreed that by eliminating warranty costs, the higher-priced gasket was in fact the lowest-cost gasket.

"Reductio ad absurdum" is Rainmaker Latin meaning "reduce to the absurd." Showing the logical extension of an ill-conceived argument can expose the weaknesses in the argument. Showing that the logical ending of an idea is absurd makes the beginning of the idea also absurd.

That's what the gasket salesperson did. He reduced the purchasing agent's gasket-buying logic to the absurd. The absurd is putting in no gasket. The point, of course, is that if it is absurd to build a transmission with no gasket, then it is a little less absurd, but absurd nonetheless, to put in a partial gasket, a gasket with a hole in it, a gasket that leaks.

Reduce to the absurd and the absurd becomes obvious.

How about just
turning off the
power to your
house to save
money?

• XXII •

Always Make That Last Call

*I*t was not a "dark and stormy night." But it was a dark and cold and sleet-filled 5:45 A.M. when the sales rep stared through the windshield wipers and thought about the two-hour drive to make his first call of the day at 8:00 A.M. To go or not to go? That was the question. He had scheduled four tough-to-get appointments. "To go" it must be. So, like the legendary postmen of yore, he sallied forth.

At 8:20 A.M., while sitting in the customer's lobby awaiting his 8:00 A.M. appointment, the receptionist took a call. The sales rep's customer was having car trouble and would not be able to make the meeting. 0 for 1. Zero batting average. Bad start. But the rep had three additional appointments at 11:00 A.M., 1:00 P.M., and 4:00 P.M. The last call was with a potential new customer, a company about which the sales rep knew little more than what was on their website.

The 11:00 A.M. sales call was another bust. The company had a factory crisis and could not pull the decision makers together. The 1:00 P.M. sales call was a bad news/good news disaster. The bad news was that the customer's plane was weather-delayed and the customer was a no-show. The good news was that the customer did not see the sleet-soaked, disheveled salesperson who had to walk half a mile through the storm from his car to the customer's office.

The salesperson now faced a three-hour wait— for what would probably be a five-minute sales call— plus a two- to three-hour drive home during the nighttime storm. To stay or not to stay? That was the new question. He debated the options: blow off the last sales call and go home; or sit in the car in sleet-soaked socks and shoes. He reviewed his precall notes on the 4:00 P.M. prospect. The company was a spark plug manufacturer. He had no idea if the spark plug company used his type of product, but the customer had agreed to see him, and that agreement is a buy signal. The only person he could get to see worked in the purchasing department, suggesting a tough, challenging, adversarial encounter. The sales rep decided. "I am," he told himself, "a selling machine. I will not be rained upon. I am the Rainmaker on this rainy day. This will not be my last call of the day; it will be the first!" So he stayed, sleet-soaked and all.

He signed the visitors' book, and was announced at 3:55 P.M. At 3:57 the head purchasing agent bounded into the lobby and said, "We are having crippling delivery performance and quality issues with our present supplier. Our chief manufacturing engineer worked with your company in a prior job. We have one question: Can you help us, and can you help us today?" At 4:06 P.M. the sales rep met with the chief manufacturing engineer and worked out a product testing procedure and test schedule. At 4:46

it was mutually agreed that if the sales rep's product worked as claimed, his company would become the new supplier. (In two weeks the sales rep received his first order for $480,000. The customer is still a customer and over the years has purchased in excess of $4,000,000.)

In a particularly poor reprise of Gene Kelly dancing in the rain, the sales rep left his new customer and danced through the sleet- and puddle-filled parking lot. The future commissions would more than cover dry cleaning and new shoes.

Always make that last call. It might turn rainwater into liquid gold.

Set to Get

*S*et goals to get goals. If you don't know where you are going, you will have a hard time getting there. If you don't know where you are going, your road map, if you have one, will be useless. If you do know where you are going, if you have a clear goal, then you can craft a plan to get there.

Just as the Rainmaker gives to get—for example, gives a sample to get a sale—so, too, the Rainmaker sets goals to get goals. Rainmaker goals are always crystal clear. The goals are always expressed in numbers. The goals are expressed in numbers so the Rainmaker can measure progress. Rainmaker goals are always sales outcomes or are tangible selling activities that, if executed well, help achieve outcomes.

In sports, outcomes are goals scored, shots made, games won. Typical Rainmaker outcome goals include annual revenues to generate, number of new accounts to add, number of actual sales closed. Rainmakers do not confuse selling strategies, even proven selling strategies, with outcomes. For example, it is a given that the more sales calls a salesperson makes, the higher the probability of making sales. But making lots of sales calls is a strategy to achieve a sales goal, such as increased revenue. The number of letters sent, phone calls made, samples delivered, seminars conducted, speeches given, are all selling strategies; they are not sales outcomes. Rainmakers always know the difference between a selling activity and a sales goal.

When salespeople blur the distinction between activities and outcomes, they set misguiding goals. For example, fund-raisers for charities and colleges and not-for-profit organizations often set goals, say, to get 50 percent or 70 percent of the class of '08 to send money to the school, or to get 45 percent of all subscribers to contribute to the City Stage Company. Such fund-raisers even give prizes or awards to people who meet such goals. But the fund-raiser's primary goal should be donations, not donors. Getting donations (i.e., money) is the desired outcome. Getting donors is a strategy. It is far less expensive to get one donor who donates $1,000,000 than to persuade one thousand donors to each donate $1,000. (Be mindful: It is also riskier to have only one donor. Having more donors lessens the risk of losing a donor and presents the opportunity to get more from each donor.)

Understanding the difference between strategies and goals is key to selling success.

Diane owned a business that sold prepared take-out lunches and dinners. Sales were good, but not great. Diane noticed that many customers visited the store and left without buying. This perplexed Diane because she prepared foods specifically requested by customers in survey after survey. Adding to her concern was that she received only praise for her products. Diane spent time training her counterpeople on how to deal with customers, and assumed they were selling. She asked her counterpeople their opinion regarding sales. One person asked Diane, "How much business should we be doing each day?" With that question Diane saw the obvious: The counterpeople had no sales goals, and no reference for success. Diane told the counterpeople that she wanted them to sell $1,000 worth of product the next day. She set a specific goal. Then Diane made it worthwhile for the counterpeople to meet the goal. Even though Diane's people were well-trained, motivated, and goal-oriented, Diane knew that everyone loves rewards. Diane said that if the team hit $1,000, everyone would get a manicure. The next day Diane's people sold $1,000, and two days later the counter flashed of perfect nails (and Joseph's nails never looked better).

Because Rainmakers set goals, they get goals. Always set to get.

• XXIV •

Take the Word "Price" Out of Your Vocabulary

Rainmakers rarely utter the word "price." This is because the word "price" is often used incorrectly by customers. Some customers (actually lots of customers) incorrectly use the word "price" as a synonym for "cost." When customers say, "I want the lowest price," they should mean they want the "lowest total cost." When the customer says he or she wants the lowest cost, the Rainmaker deliberately takes the customer literally and works to give the customer the lowest cost . . . regardless of product price.

Price is but one of the many factors that all add up to the true cost of a product. To illustrate, a customer is considering buying a car and is choosing between two. One car is *priced* at $20,000, the other at $25,000. Which car costs more, the one priced at $20,000 or the one priced at $25,000? To calculate the true cost of each car, you must sum each car's initial purchase price *plus* its maintenance costs, fuel usage, insurance, financing costs, property taxes, resale value, depreciation. Thus, if the $20,000 car incurs an additional $5,000 per year in maintenance costs, after three years the car's total cost is $35,000. If the $25,000 car incurs annual costs of $2,000, then that car's three-year cost is $31,000. The highest-priced car is the lowest-cost car.

Which instrument costs more, the lower-priced instrument or the higher-priced? Which laboratory test costs more . . . which transmission costs more . . . which furnace costs more . . . which lawnmower costs more? The answer, of course, is, the customer does not know. However, if the only thing the customer hears is price, then price could be the determining purchase factor. The Rainmaker always presents price as one element of total cost. The Rainmaker always educates the customer to the total value received from investing in the product.

There are customers who are price cutters and customers who are cost cutters. The Rainmaker likes to work with cost cutters. Customers who buy only on the lowest price, and who disregard the negative cost consequences associated with such myopic buying, should be avoided if they can't be educated. There is an old saying that certain customers know the price of everything and the value of nothing. These customers have not yet been educated by a Rainmaker. If you must deal with such a customer, ask him or her to help you calculate how much a new car actually costs. After the car comparison drill, they usually get the message.

If a customer asks, "What is the price?", give the price. (Eighty-two percent of customers who ask for the price simply want to know the price. They are not negotiating.) After giving the price, ask, "How does that sound?" If you get a response such as, "Are you kidding? That's way more than I thought," follow up by asking, "May I show you why this product is actually the lowest-cost solution to your problem?" Then proceed to show the customer how the investment in your product so reduces the customer's costs, or increases revenues, or both, that price is a mere detail. Never let the purchasing conversation be about price when it should be about cost. Take "price" out of your vocabulary. Don't replace the word "price" with the word "cost"; they mean different things. Replace "price" with "investment." This will help you educate the customer and improve the customer's vocabulary.

Make an Offer They Can't Refuse

*O*ne of the great lines in one of the great movies is when the Godfather, Don Corleone, referring to a reluctant business associate who makes motion pictures, tells his consigliere, "I'll make him an offer he can't refuse." The Godfather ultimately gains complete cooperation from the reluctant business associate. Movie fans know that Rainmakers don't have the same "powers of persuasion" as did the Godfather. However, Rainmakers can make an offer so good, smart customers won't refuse.

This "can't refuse" offer is a powerful, compelling proposition.

For legitimate reasons, customers are often tentative about buying a new (to them) product or service. This is especially true when the investment is large and the results promised by the product can't be completely ascertained until *after* the product is purchased. Consider companies that sell a combination of products and services that reduce their customers' overall electricity costs, or consumption of cutting tools, or water usage, or maintenance costs. In these kinds of cases, in order to realize the cost saving (or whatever the economic benefits may be), the customer has to first invest money in the seller's products and services. Many potential customers are justifiably concerned if investing in the seller's product is the correct decision to make. One sales strategy to help the customer make the correct decision, and to buy, is to make the customer an offer they won't refuse.

To get the customer to invest, and to get the customer a positive dollar return on that investment, the Rainmaker makes this offer: "Authorize us to conduct a detailed cost reduction audit of your electricity usage [or cutting tool usage, or water usage, or product return costs, or warranty claims, or whatever]. Your investment in that comprehensive cost reduction audit will be $25,000. Here are three fail-safe options for you to choose:

"One, if we cannot find ways to save you at least $200,000, the audit is free, no charge, and you get all our cost reduction ideas for free.

"Or two, if we do find $200,000 in documented savings and *you go ahead* with the proposal, you will get the $25,000 audit fee rebated to you.

"Or three, if we find $200,000 in documented savings, and you don't go ahead, you pay the $25,000 audit fee and you get all of our cost reduction ideas for free.*

"You have nothing to lose. Why not give the proposal a try?"

If the customer is a good company, and is inter-

---

*Giving away the cost reduction ideas is smart. If the customer were, in the future, to implement the ideas, it is likely the customer would need to buy the seller's products to do the implementation.

ested in reducing costs or improving its financial situation, then this is an offer the customer won't refuse.

Presented clearly and fairly, a triple-outcome offer is one that good customers will consider because there are built-in safety nets. Good, qualified customers will understand this is an offer they shouldn't refuse.

Grazie mille, Godfather.

• XXVI •
Never Let Anyone Outwork You

Too many sales managers attempt to spur on their salespeople with the cliché "work smarter, not harder." Whatever does "work smarter, not harder" mean? Without task-specific coaching, teaching, training, how does someone instantly get smarter? Does one take fish oil capsules or eat spinach? And what do you do if you are as smart as you are ever going to get? And, uh-oh, uh-oh, what if you are dumber? What if the other guy or gal is smarter, taller, faster, better-looking, more articulate? What do you do? You can't quit. You can't hide. You can't give in.

You work harder. Here's how:

- Ask for one more referral.
- Send one more letter.
- Spend more time precall planning.
- Craft more questions to ask.
- Practice asking the questions.
- Role play.
- Make a plan, work the plan.
- Use every minute in every day.
- Make one more phone call or sales call.
- Ask for the order.
- Keep knocking on the door.
- Do it again tomorrow.

Try to get smarter. But don't wait until you get smarter. You can get smarter by doing something *today*. Pick up the phone. Pick up the pencil. Do something right now. Compete for inches. Work harder.

You can't control the other guy. You can't control

how many calls, how much practice, how much self-learning the other guy will do. But you can control yourself. You can control your work ethic, your attitude, your professionalism, your schedule. Therefore, never, never let the other guy outwork you.

• XXVII •

Always Attempt a "One-Call" Close

No matter how big the deal; no matter how complex the solution; no matter how long the historical sales cycle; always plan and prepare to close the sale on call number one. Always attempt to make that first sales call on the highest-level decision maker. Always know how much money you are going to make the customer. Always know the economic consequences to the customer if the customer does not buy from you. Always ask for the order, or for a customer commitment to an action that leads directly to the sale.

It is OK if you don't get the sale on the first call. One-call closes are uncommon, particularly for products or services that require a significant customer investment. But it is not OK to prejudge the customer's buying attitude and to assume a traditional long sales cycle, and then to sell the same old way. Never assume that the way everyone has always sold, and that the way every customer has always bought, is the way it must be. For example, if you and your customer agree that the net dollarized value of your solution is $365,000, then it costs the customer $1,000 a day to go without your solution. When the customer sees $1,000 a day go down the sewer, it tends to shorten the sales cycle, and perhaps shorten the cycle to one call.

· XXVIII ·

Influence the Influencers

Many people buy products because people other than the salesperson influenced them to buy the product. Kids buy a brand of basketball shoes because LeBron James, the National Basketball Association phenom, wears the brand, and not because of a shoe salesman. LeBron James is an influencer. Star athletes are obvious influencers. So, too, are movie stars, theater critics, restaurant reviewers. Other influencers are friends, coaches, teachers, mentors, television pundits, newspaper editors, wine writers, bartenders, advisers, trendsetters, role models, parents, specification writers, customer colleagues, novelists, concierges. Influencers abound, and getting influential people to sell your product, to suggest your product, to endorse your product, to use your product, to say your product's brand name is smart strategy.

The liquor industry and the cigarette industry have long used influence strategies because they were denied access to television advertising. Soda pop sellers want their cans and bottles front and center in every hit television show. Fashion designers want the hip new actress to flaunt a gown on every red carpet in Hollywood. Pharmaceutical companies influence doctors to prescribe their medications. Window makers influence architects to design buildings with their windows. Medical products companies influence medical textbooks to influence future doctors. Great musicians influence ambitious musicians. Engineering products companies do the same for engineering textbooks. Lobbyists influence lawmakers to make laws that favor their clients.

She owned a hair salon. One of her clients was an

assistant coach of a National Hockey League team. She offered the assistant coach a free haircut for every hockey player he influenced to visit her salon. Soon she was swamped with hockey players. The hockey players influenced their girlfriends and wives to visit the salon. Soon single women, hoping to meet single hockey players, visited the salon. Then hockey-playing kids influenced their moms to take them to the salon in hopes of glimpsing a hero. One influencer influenced another influencer, who influenced others. Hockey pucks to haircuts. Ka-ching, ka-ching!

Influencing the influencers is smart rainmaking. Smart Rainmakers are happy to let the influencers do the Rainmaker's job. Rainmakers don't care how they get the sale, or who gets credit for the sale, as long as they get paid for the sale. So, find the influencers, influence the influencers, and hear that cash register ring.

• XXIX •

Silence Is Golden

*M*ost salespeople talk too much during sales
calls. They talk, talk, talk, and tell, tell, tell,
instead of asking questions and letting the customer
talk. One Rainmaker secret is that during any sales
call the customer should do 80 percent of the talking. Therefore, in a thirty-minute sales call the customer should be talking for twenty-four minutes.
Letting the customer talk, and listening hard to what
the customer is saying, takes self-discipline. Listening also requires great questions, as the art of listening

starts with the art of questioning. In a thirty-minute sales call, when the Rainmaker speaks, he or she is asking questions and offering benefits and points of difference.

Reining in the urge to talk is tough for the bright, passionate, energetic salesperson. But it is the bright and passionate salespeople who become Rainmakers. These people love their products, love their companies, love their customers, and love their job of selling. They can find it difficult to curb their fervor and enthusiasm and let the customer participate, but curb their fervor they must.

One Rainmaker constantly battled to talk less and listen more. He knew the 80 percent listening rule. He knew that as his share of the conversation in a sales call went up, his probability of achieving his sales call objective went down. He knew his propensity to talk too much was hurting his results, and then one day he really learned the lesson. He scheduled a lunch meeting with a prospective client who was looking for someone to do a market research project. The night before the meeting the market research account executive (the salesman) was stricken with a wicked sore throat, but no other symptoms. Rescheduling would have pushed the sales call months into the future, jeopardizing the chance of getting the project. (And in selling, the future is now.) At the lunch the client's two representatives were chatty, animated, excited about the importance of the research. Because of his sore throat, the account executive (AE) did uncharacteristically little talking. His participation was limited to taking notes, giving encouraging smiles, and knowing nods of the noggin. The client representatives asked the AE questions, but before he could croak out an answer, they answered their own questions. Finally, one of the client reps said the AE's company was obviously qualified. The other client rep asked the AE how much the research project would cost to complete. Before the AE could whisper "Twenty-five thousand dollars," the client blurted, "Our budget for the project is forty thousand dollars." Then before the AE could say "OK," the customer said, "OK, forty-five thousand dollars, but that's it, OK?" "OK," answered the account executive, an answer that soothed his sore throat.

Lesson learned. Silence sells. Silence made the sale, and for $20,000 more than the seller expected. Be a seller, not a teller. Be a "sell guy," not a "tell guy." Pauses and periods of silence are powerful selling weapons.

"Shush-s-s-s-h!"

• XXX •

Never Give a Quote

*E*xcept in rare instances, such as certain types of government contract sales, don't present your price as a quote. The word "quote" is a synonym for "price." Never present your price on a quotation form. Never invest a lot of time and energy to respond to RFQs (Requests for Quotation). Never invest time and money to respond to RFPs (Requests for Proposal). To do so is to confirm to the requester that your product is an undifferentiated commodity. If you feel you must respond to an RFQ, take five minutes, put in a profitable price, send, and forget. Unless you are devoid of imagination and creativity (but because you are reading this book, you are surely not devoid of imagination), then your product or service is not a commodity, regardless of what your "customer" would like you to believe.

If you have a differentiated product, then simply quoting a price assumes you think the customer knows your dollarized value proposition. This is wrong-minded. Customers who buy via quotes almost always have no clue as to your dollarized value. They incorrectly assume that all suppliers supply the same product, have equal technical support, deliver in the exact same time frame, have equivalent personnel. Don't fall into the quotation or RFP trap. Your job is to find a way around the RFP, and to educate the customer to your points of difference and to your true quantified value.

Customers who buy solely on the basis of the lowest price are always low-profit or no-profit customers. Sellers that bother to respond to RFQs should check their sales success history. They will find that such impersonal, over the phone or electronic bids, which are based only on low price, result in a capture rate of zero to 15 percent. That means for every one hundred quotes, the seller wins the sale zero to fifteen times. And those zero to fifteen sales will be at barely profitable low prices. Those zero to fifteen customers will be very high maintenance. They will unceasingly insist on concessions, better terms, add-ons, extras. They will never be loyal. They will drop you for a nickel. They will divert you from getting and keeping good customers. And sooner or later your low-price bid to zero to fifteen customers will become the standard for all.

Playing this bad game means you don't have competitive points of difference, or you don't know your true value, or you don't know how to articulate and sell that value. These are losing scenarios. Reinvest the time and money spent on quoting and filling out ten-plus-page RFQs into innovation, marketing, and selling skills training.

If your marketplace has so deteriorated that all customers refuse to recognize value, or are closed to innovation, and you wish to continue selling to these customers, then try these selling strategies. Offer to write all or part of the RFQ. Tilt the RFQ to favor your products. Write all or part of the product specifications. Add innovative ideas that cannot be summarily ignored, even by the dimmest of customers. Calculate the potential economic consequences to the customer of not going with your product, and include that dollar number in your proposal.

Always change the ground rules (of the RFQ) and do so in ways that are legitimately helpful to the customer.

Quote your dollarized value. Quote Shakespeare or Bob Dylan or Dylan Thomas. Quote the Bible or Bartlett's or Thomas Jefferson. But don't quote your price.

Killer Sales Questions
#3 and #4

Often during a sales call the customer will ask a
seemingly innocuous question, or ask what an
ordinary salesperson might consider to be a trivial
technical question. For example, the customer might
ask, "Does your product come in four-gallon jugs?"
or "What metals can your product coat?" The ordinary salesperson will often launch into a long answer
either accentuating what the salesperson believes
are the positives, or neutralizing what the salesperson guesses may be some negatives implied by the

customer's question. Not so the Rainmaker. The Rainmaker answers the questions as succinctly and factually as possible. For example, to answer the customer's question about the four-gallon jugs, the Rainmaker will begin his or her answer with, "Yes, it does," or "No, it doesn't," or "I don't know." Then the Rainmaker will always complete the answer with the killer sales question "Why do you ask?" To answer the customer's question about the metals the product can coat, the Rainmaker responds, "Our product coats at least thirty different metals. Why do you ask?"

"Why do you ask?" is a killer sales question. ⟵

The Rainmaker knows that in this busy world decision makers rarely ask idle, unimportant questions. The Rainmaker knows that customer questions are often "buy signals." This is why the great salesperson probes to determine the customer's real need, particularly if that need is hidden within a simple question.

When the customer answers the killer question "Why do you ask?", the Rainmaker now knows at least one important customer issue. For example, the customer might answer, "In our fabrication process, we have ten different metals that need coating. I'd prefer to have one company that could supply all ten coatings." Then the Rainmaker asks the second killer sales question: "How important is it to you to have one supplier?"

Depending on the degree of importance having one supplier is to the customer, the Rainmaker can immediately ask for a commitment. For example, if the customer answers, "Extremely important," then the Rainmaker says, "Our product will coat all your metals. What does it take to test the coating on your metals?"

The twin killer sales questions "Why do you ask?" and "How important is that to you?" encourage the customer to talk about the specifics of their need, the seriousness of their need, the budget to solve it, and the timetable.

These are two simple questions always asked by Rainmakers, never asked by ordinary salespeople. Asking these two questions is one simple selling secret.

prospective customer the salesperson is both polite
and persistent, the salesperson can call on a customer for as long as it takes—up to an introduction,
to get an appointment, to a demonstration, or to
get an order.

Being persistent—continuing to call—after the
customer won't respond to your letters, won't take
your calls, won't give you an appointment, won't
give you a chance, just isn't in the business, and then
come on, it is natural to simply put off and go after
other opportunities. However, if the customer is
worth the wait, with the pursuit, that amount
yourself to stay in the hunt. I'll see persistence often

• XXXII •

Politeness + Persistence =
Performance

*E*verybody knows a salesperson is supposed to be persistent: to keep calling, keep knocking on doors, never give up. That's great, but if a salesperson is only persistent, the customer will see the salesperson as insistent, as annoying, as an irritant. And everybody knows that a salesperson should always be polite, considerate, courteous. If, in his or her dealings with a prospective customer, the salesperson is only polite, he or she will be a disappointed and hungry salesperson. But if in pursuing a prospective customer the salesperson is both polite and persistent, the salesperson can call on a customer for as long as it takes to get an introduction, to get an appointment, to get a demonstration, or to get an order.

Being persistent is not easy. If time after time the customer won't respond to your letters, won't take your calls, won't give you an appointment, won't give you a chance, promises to do business and then reneges, it is natural to write the guy off and go after other opportunities. However, if the customer is worth the wait, worth the pursuit, then motivate yourself to stay in the hunt. Patient persistence often pays off.

Staying polite is not always easy. It is difficult to stay polite and mannerly when the customer blows off a meeting and doesn't tell you, or rudely leaves you waiting, or doesn't do what was promised, or even says "You are hired" and doesn't hire you or buy from you. It is hard to stay polite when the customer asks other companies to quote a price based on your ideas, on your design, or is happy to have you take him out to lunch or dinner or a ballgame, and gives the other guy his business. But if the business is worth it, you must be unflaggingly polite.

Being polite does not mean being timid. Being polite is not an excuse for not asking the customer questions. It is polite and correct and OK to ask a customer how he or she is compensated; to ask their goals; to ask about their concerns and problems; to ask their expectations. It is polite to ask for the sale, for customer commitments, for the order.

There are customers who may want to do business with you, but for good reasons cannot. They may not tell you this, and their stalling and deadline missing and unreturned calls may appear to be noninterest. If you quit too soon, you won't get the business.

Good customers appreciate patient, polite, persistent pursuers. Good customers appreciate salespeople who bump into a customer stonewall and ask permission to call again sometime. Good customers are flattered that good salespeople want to do business with them.

Persistent polite salespeople always preplan every contact with the elusive customer. They always think of something new to show; always give the customer some takeaway. They always make it worthwhile for the customer to spend even three minutes on the phone.

Politeness plus persistence is an irresistible selling style. Politeness plus persistence is powerful. Politeness plus persistence is a formula for positive sales performance.

Thank you. Is it OK if I call you again?

Always Take Notes

Subway — what kind of cheese?

C ustomers don't care about you, but they expect you to care about them. Customers expect you to be prepared when you meet them. Customers expect you to ask prepared questions. They expect you to take notes. Taking notes demonstrates that you care. Not taking notes tells the customer you do not care about what the customer is saying. When the customer is talking, and you are not taking notes, the customer is thinking, "Why am I bothering with this person? This guy can't remember everything. He will definitely get something wrong. My view isn't important. He is not a pro. Let's cut the conversation short."

The restaurant was popular, trendy, expensive. The waitstaff was twenty-ish to thirty-ish, hip, attractive men and women. Given the volume of customers, and the high menu prices, waiters and waitresses could earn $150 to $300 in gratuities a night, and occasionally a good deal more.

Every Monday the restaurant manager held a "sales meeting" with the waitstaff. They discussed techniques on selling more after-dinner drinks, more desserts, more specials. They discussed dealing with the VIP customer, the lingering-too-long-at-the-table customer, the obnoxious customer, the repeat customer. They talked about how to sell more food and drink, generating more tips, which was a win/win for the restaurant and the waitstaff.

It was no secret as to the approximate amount of tip money each waiter and waitress and bartender made each week. The manager was intrigued that one waitress consistently trailed her colleagues in earning tips. She was bright, personable, likable. But she made less money. She had the same number of tables, the same number of customers. What was she not doing, or what was she doing wrong? After observation, the answer was obvious: The under-earning waitress did not write down the customers' orders. She memorized the orders. The waitress thought she was impressing the customers by memorizing the orders and then—voilà!—accurately serving the various dishes and drinks. But instead of impressing customers, she made them anxious. Even when she got the orders right, she created unnecessary customer angst because the customer anticipated that she *might* make a mistake. And, of course, any mistake, no matter how small or uncommon, was magnified because it was a mistake that the customer believed could have been prevented. She was making less money because she wasn't taking notes when her customers were talking. After some advice, she started writing down orders, taking notes, keeping her customers relaxed, taking the spotlight off herself, and she started to see bigger tips and bonus tips.

Take handwritten notes on every sales call.

Don't use a laptop (and, God forbid, never plop your laptop atop a customer's desk or table). Don't borrow a pen. Don't borrow paper. Bring both. Summarize your notes into a follow-up report to the customer. Write the summary to positively enhance your position. Wield the power of the pen.

Turn sales call notes into bank notes, into legal tender, into rain.

Love this!

• XXXIV •

How to Conduct a Needs Analysis

You can't help a customer until you know what he or she needs. You can't provide a solution until you know the problem to solve. Determining what a customer needs to improve his or her situation is crucial to ultimately helping the customer. Doctors diagnose a customer (aka patient) problem by asking questions ("Where does it hurt?") and by administering tests. Rainmakers diagnose a customer's problem by asking questions and listening intently to the answers. Asking a customer thirty, forty, fifty questions is called a needs analysis. Rainmakers always conduct in-depth needs analysis.

There are practical problems in conducting a needs analysis. First, you must know the questions you will ask. You have to ask the questions in some order. You have to keep track of the questions asked. You have to take notes on the customer's answers. You have to juggle questions, answers, customer tangents, new areas of investigation.

Here are some secrets to conducting a sales-getting needs analysis:

1. In precall planning, write out every question you intend to ask.
2. Group those questions that seem related by inquiry area (e.g., determining who the decision makers are requires four or five related questions).
3. Organize the questions in the best chronological order you can.
4. Divide your notebook pages with a vertical line, not down the middle but approximately

at one-third of the page from the right margin. On the right side of the dividing line, write out all your questions, preceding each with a check-off box ☐. The space to the left of the dividing line is for your notes. Your notebook pages will appear as below.

NOTES:	
	Client Name _____
	Date _____
	☐ What are your goals?
	☐ What are your challenges?
	☐ What solutions have you tried?
	☐ What is the problem costing you?
	☐ What are the consequences if the problem continues?
	☐ What is your timetable?
	☐ What is your budget?
	☐ Who else are you talking to?
	☐ Who, in addition to yourself, will be involved in choosing a supplier?
	☐ What are their concerns?

When you ask a question, check the box. Be sure all boxes are checked. You will have completed a rare, successful needs analysis.

In the age of the laptop, the computerized calendar, the computerized daily meeting schedule, the computerized everything, this interview strategy is so simple, so yesterday, that it will stay a secret from those who don't read this book.

• XXXV •

How to Prepare
a Presentation

*L*ots of salespeople think that presentations are
selling events. Rarely, if ever, are presentations
effective selling events. Presentations don't sell. People sell. Thus, Rainmakers rarely give presentations.
Too many salespeople rely on PowerPoint presentations to make the sale. It is certain that in the near future some PowerPointers will be arrested on felony
charges for trying to bore their customers to death.
Most sales call presentations are dreadful. The presentations are too often all about the presenters—their

credentials, their company history, their philosophy. No customer cares about such puffery. The customer already knows enough about you to invite you. Most presentations are not 100 percent about the customer (which is 100 percent of the customer's interest). Most presentations are too long, too wordy, too complex, too boring. Most presentations incorrectly give the seller's price on the last, or second-to-last slide, instead of on the first or second slide.

Most presenters finish their presentation, give a tentative glance at the audience, don't ask for the order, and hope the customer is going to leap to her feet and clasp her hands in delight, exclaiming, "What a great presentation! Loved the charts. We'll sign up right this minute." That ain't gonna happen. Futile hope.

If there must be a presentation, and if the presentation is intended to get business, to be a sales call, here is how the presentation should be structured.

Slide 1. Briefly summarize what benefits the customer will get from the presenter. It is best if those benefits are dollarized.

For example, Slide 1 might read:

GOAL

How ABC Company can increase production yields by 2%, generating $6,000,000 in scrap reduction and $1,500,000 in new revenues.

Slide 2. This slide outlines the investment ABC Company must make (to get the $7,500,000), and summarizes where that investment is spent.

For example, Slide 2 might read:

OPPORTUNITY

To realize $6,000,000 in new savings and $1,500,000 in new revenues, ABC Company should invest $700,000 in down-line centrifuges.

Slide 3. This slide lists what the presenter believes will be customer objections to buying the centrifuges. The objections were uncovered in precall homework and in needs analysis. However, the objections are not presented as the customer might voice them. They are presented as mutual customer/ seller objectives. For example, a possible customer objection might be, "Your deliveries are always late. You are never on schedule." This objection would appear on the slide (titled "Project Objectives") as, "To insure that the centrifuges are delivered when and where ABC Company wants."

If there were other possible objections such as high price, reliability concerns, and after-sale service, Slide 3 might read as follows:

PROJECT OBJECTIVES

- On-time centrifuges delivery
- Competitive pricing
- Positive dollar return on investment
- Noninterruptible service
- Uptime service within 24 hours

Slide 4. This slide summarizes the customer's problems and needs. For example, Slide 4 might read:

PRESENT SITUATION
- 3% of potential output wasted
- Yield problem occurs 4 steps downstream
- Yield problem occurs in high-value phase
- Higher-yield product can be sold at full price. Revenue opportunity.
- No solution being tested

Slide 5. This slide summarizes the presenter's recommendations, which, if followed, lead to a sale. For example, Slide 5 might read:

ACTION PLAN
- Form joint-company project team
- Develop implementation schedule
- Lab-test new centrifuges
- Test full-size centrifuges
- Install centrifuges into process system

After reviewing Slide 5, the presenter asks the decision maker(s), "Who from ABC Company should be on the project team?" This is asking for a customer commitment that leads to a sale.

This type of presentation is not a surrogate salesperson. This presentation is simply a sales aid used by the salesperson to help make the sale. Every forty- , fifty- , and sixty-slide presentation can be pruned to fewer than ten slides. Ten slides is better than eleven slides.

If the presentation you use now requires a warning, "Do not drive heavy machinery or jog on a treadmill while watching this presentation," that is a clue that you are jeopardizing the health of your customer and killing your chance to make the sale.

Presentation P.S.: Please kill any slides that have your company logo shaking hands with the customer's logo, or any kind of handshaking partnership visual cliché. Customers feel those shaking hands around their throat, choking them.

Relationships Are Bunk

Yeah, yeah, yeah, everyone knows "relationships" are important in selling. Everyone thinks that relationships are critical to selling. All the old boys extol the virtues of relationships. All the books tell salespeople to "build relationships." Fine. Good. But know one thing: Depend on relationships to make the sale at your peril. Depend on relationships to fund your paycheck, and you will be one hungry salesperson. When it comes to getting the sale, relationships are bunk.

If there are a million salespeople who build good

relationships with customers, then there are a million definitions of "relationship." Assume a good relationship between a customer and a salesperson has at least the following elements: They know each other, trust each other, understand each other, like each other, have done business together or will in the future, have profited from each other, have had a beer together. That's all great. But when it comes to the next sale, a relationship is absolutely no guarantee that the salesperson will get the sale, or even be considered as a possible supplier.

Claiming a relationship is a conceit. It is one way salespeople validate their past selling and past customer-service efforts. Claiming a relationship is sometimes used as a surrogate in place of getting the sale, as in "Well, we didn't win this one, but we've got a great relationship." Claiming relationships is sometimes a subtle salesperson excuse for not asking the customer in-depth questions, or not asking for the order.

Putting too much trust in the strength of a relationship leads to mistakes. The ordinary salesperson may take something for granted. The Rainmaker takes nothing for granted. The ordinary salesperson may feel that diligent precall planning on a relationship customer is not necessary. The salesperson may get complacent, nonchalant, overconfident. The salesperson may feel that he or she knows all the answers, and does not keep asking questions. Rainmakers treat every customer like a new customer. Rainmakers treat every customer as if the relationship were in jeopardy.

Here are some common clues that indicate the sacred relationship may not be ringing the cash register:

- The customer buys something you sell from someone else.
- The customer says, "I didn't know you guys sold or did such and such."
- The customer's warehouse, or tool crib, or retail shelf, or testing lab, or driveway is filled with the other guy's products.
- The customer says, "Don't take this the wrong way, but . . . the new guy wants to review all contracts . . . we want to see what else is out there . . . a very good company has made an interesting proposal. . . ."

A relationship can get you into the game for a new opportunity. A relationship gets you the "last look" at the pricing in a competitive situation. A relationship gets you the deal when all else is seen as equal. These are important selling advantages and must never be neglected or disregarded. But a relationship does not make the sale, guarantee the sale, or allow the salesperson to take it easy, saunter in, and pick up the order.

The relationship is only as solid as the dollarized value of the personal and business benefits the customer has received from the seller and the seller's organization. Thus, the relationship must be re-earned every day. The relationship is not a given, it is not a crutch, it is not a good luck charm . . . it is one factor in the selling calculus.

Definitely strive to get and cement relationships. Invest in the relationships. Nurture the relationships. But don't bank on the relationships. The prudent, objective Rainmaker knows that seller-to-customer relationships are under stress, fragile, ephemeral, vulnerable. "Relationships" as a bankable selling strategy is bunk.

Don't bank on bunk.

• XXXVII •

Please Pass the "P's"

A Rainmaker's personality is pleasantly peppered with this pack of "P's."

- Passion. Rainmakers love their lives.
- Paid. Rainmakers make the most money.
- Persevere. Rainmakers are tougher than tough times.
- Persistent. Rainmakers don't quit.
- Physically Phit. Rainmakers look after themselves. The body carries the brain.

- Play. Rainmakers have phun.
- Polished. Rainmakers pay attention at knife and fork school. Polished manners, polished nails, polished shoes, polished cars.
- Polite. Rainmakers are polite to everyone. Nice costs nothing.
- Precall planners. Rainmakers preplan every single sales call.
- Prepared. Rainmakers are *"Semper Paratus."* (See "Rainmaker Mottos," Chapter III.)
- Price to value. Rainmakers sell the dollarized value of what customers get, and price to that value.
- Problem solvers. Rainmakers make their customers happy.
- Produce, perform. Rainmakers make rain. They sell. They ring the cash register.
- Professional. Rainmakers are professional in all selling areas, big and small.
- Prompt. Rainmakers are fast.

- Proud. Rainmakers are public patriots for their company, customers, and products.
- Punctual. Rainmakers are always early, never late.

products.

• XXXVIII •

Sell the Resellers

Rainmakers love resellers. Resellers are the people who sell the Rainmaker's products or services to end users. Resellers are known by various names. Resellers are distributors, wholesalers, auctioneers, retailers, dealerships, integrators, VARs (the acronym for "value added reseller," which is the term some technology companies hyperbolically call their distributors). Resellers are the people who make the sale, or take an order, from those end-user customers on whom the Rainmaker rarely calls.

Rainmakers love resellers because resellers can leverage the Rainmaker, expand the Rainmaker's selling capacity. This selling capacity is often called "feet on the street." If a Rainmaker signs up a distributor with twenty-five salespeople to resell his or her product, then that Rainmaker has a potential new selling asset of twenty-five people on the street selling.

Here are some secrets that Rainmakers use to help resellers sell more:

1. Have low expectations. Resellers represent many products and allocate their selling time over all products. And, sadly, many reseller salespeople are poor sellers, order takers at best. Don't expect all the feet on the street to pound the pavement for you; expect one or two, or maybe three.

2. Find that salesperson(s) in the reseller's organization who can sell, and spend all your training time with that person(s) and with nobody else.

3. If your product deserves 5 percent of the reselling organization's selling time, work to

get 7 percent. Do this with training, personal attention, focus, motivation, incentives, joint sales calls.

4. Resellers will make you money, but you must make them money first. Assume a reseller is not going to make the first sale on a new customer because 98 percent of the time they won't. The Rainmaker makes the first sale, and the reseller will make the second, third, fourth, and eighth resale.

5. Don't abdicate the missionary selling, the brand building, the pricing to the reseller. Those roles are Rainmaker roles.

6. Teach reseller salespeople how to recognize the "clues and cues" that signal a possible sales opportunity for your products. When they find a selling clue, have the salesperson call you to help make the sale. (A good idea that helps reseller salespeople is to give them printed cards of your clues and cues.)

7. The reseller knows the account; you know your product and technology. On joint calls,

the reseller introduces you to the decision makers, and then you make the sale.

8. Dollarize your value to the reseller. The owner of the reselling company wants revenues, profits, return on assets, "drag along" sales (of other product lines), customer retention. The salespeople want compensation, commissions, recognition, praise, training. Show the reseller owner how much money your products will make the company, and show the street salesperson how much in commissions he or she will make on your products, and you will get their attention.

9. Get agreement on sales goals guidelines. Get consensus with the owner that they can resell $3,000,000 worth of products in one year. Get consensus with the salespeople that "Wednesday is Walker Widgets Day," and on Wednesdays they will concentrate on Walker Widgets.

10. Target. Tell. Show. Sell. Resell. Set target

sales goals for targeting end-use customers.
Tell resellers how and why to sell. Show them
how to sell. Sell something for them. Resell
something. Repeat.

Love resellers. Love selling the resellers.

• XXXIX •

Personalize, Personalize,
Personalize

*W*hether you are a one-person firm and you are
responsible for generating all your company's
revenues, or you are one salesperson in a sales force
of 10,000, to your customers you are the face of
your company. Customers "buy" you before they buy
your company or your products. You are a branded
package. You stand for something. Everything you do
or say, how you look, how you talk or write, is part
of your brand personality. It is how customers think

about you. And all of your persona is part of you, the person, the salesperson, the brand.

To reinforce your brand, to stay top of mind with your customers, to be memorable, you must personalize what you do as much as possible. Use your picture, if its use is tasteful and if using a picture works to reinforce your brand. Personally sign holiday cards. Send handwritten notes. Announce your name when leaving a voice mail, even if you call the customer twice a day. To someone you know, you can leave your phone number early in the voice mail. To someone you don't know, be sure to say your name slowly at the start and end of your call. Do the same with your telephone number.

Personally signed notes connect more with customers than company-signed notes. For years the head of a small advertising agency sent Christmas and holiday gifts to important clients. For years the gift card was signed in the corporate name of the agency, not by the agency head herself. For years the agency head would marvel at the spotty "thank you" responses she received, given how polite and well-mannered her clients were. One year the gift card was signed in her name. She not only received personal thank-you notes from every client, but also was invited to talk about increased business. People can't thank a company. People thank people in the company.

The personal touch is still compelling. Don't let the electronic devices that dominate interpersonal communication cause you to lose your touch. You are a person. Your customer is a person. So personalize.

Your personal touch might be your Midas touch.

• XL •

Build Customer Value Files

The first rule for a salesperson to grow his or her territory, or market, or business, or book of accounts, is not to lose business. It is hard to grow a sales territory by 10 percent if you lose business. To grow 10 percent you must first replace the lost business with new business, and then go out and get even more new business. Losing some business is inevitable and uncontrollable (for example, a good account moves out of your market, or your client contact gets fired, or your customer's product is redesigned, obsoleting your product). But much of attrition or lost business is predictable, controllable, and keepable.

If you have customers that you define as "must keep/at risk," then you must have a "customer value file" for each of those customers. "Must keep" customers are those that, if lost, will really hurt. Generally, "must keep" customers are high-revenue customers. "At risk" customers are those whose contract is ending; who are looking at other suppliers; who feel they are not getting from you what they can get from others; who are being aggressively wooed by someone else.

A "customer value file" (CVF) is a great customer "keep" tool. The CVF is a complete, detailed, quantitative history of the value, services, and activities you and your company have provided to the customer. The CVF records what you did for the customer last week and what you did ten years ago. The CVF summarizes all of the dollarized value you have provided your customer. If you reduced warranty claims by ½ percent, saving $100,000, and enabled a new product to generate $400,000 in gross margin, you are worth up to $500,000 to your customer. Your

CVF would tally the value of all engineering visits, free tests, free samples, discounted prototypes, training sessions, unreimbursed travel on behalf of the customer, and all the other services given to the customer.

Your CVF should also give a detailed, quantitative snapshot of your business relationship. If favorable to you, include how many parts shipped, or engineering hours invested, or transactions executed. Show the small percentage, if any, of defective parts. Show how many shipments made, and what percent were on time. Detail everything that demonstrates your importance to the customer.

Your CVF should include a "Milestone" section that recaptures all the big and unique contributions you provided the customer. For example, a major bearing manufacturer's CVF for an automobile OEM (original equipment manufacturer) customer recorded all the innovations the bearing company had provided the automobile company going back to 1946. With decades of innovation the automobile-maker customer could correctly infer that with so many past breakthroughs, future innovations were possible. In addition, the bearing company's employees had bought or leased 629 of the customer's cars. That kind of supplier loyalty goes a long way with any customer.

Your job is to make your customer money. How much money you saved your customer, or generated for your customer, is the heart of the customer value file.

Keeping customers is the first step to growing your business.

• XLI •

Call on Marketing

Unless you sell directly to the consumer or end
user, you are selling to a company that resells
your product as received, or uses your product as a
component in the manufacturing of their product
and then sells that finished product to their customer. For example, companies that resell your product are retail stores, mass merchandising chains,
wholesalers, distributors, value added resellers (VARs).
Customers that buy your product as a component are

original equipment manufacturers (OEMs) and system integrators.

Whether you sell to a reseller or to an OEM, the only reason they are buying your product is to make money. They consider the price they pay for a product to be an investment, and they expect a dollarized cash return on that investment.

When a retailer buys and displays, for example, eight shelf feet of greeting cards, or ten bags of barbecue charcoal, or a pallet of sparkling water, that retailer expects to resell the greeting cards for more money than it invested, or paid for the cards. When a retailer installs end-aisle displays full of greeting cards, it expects to sell more cards. When a wholesaler buys a product for $10, they expect to resell it for $13.50. When an OEM buys a bearing to put into the wheel housing it sells, that OEM expects the bearing to make its wheel housing better. "Better" means the wheel housing will be lighter, quieter, stronger, less costly, or something that will make the wheel housing more marketable, more sellable. With the "better" bearing, the wheel housing company can sell more wheel housings, or make more profit on the wheel housings they sell.

Most salespeople call on the purchasing department. Buyers who work in purchasing departments care only about getting the lowest price. Too often, buyers neither care nor are compensated for buying a product that will increase their company's sales, profits, customer satisfaction. They are paid simply to get suppliers to lower their price.

Rainmakers call on those people who care about selling *more* greeting cards, *more* wheel housings. Rainmakers call on marketing people. Marketing people are those people who are responsible for increasing sales, introducing new products, protecting product pricing, defeating competition, reducing warranty problems, building customer loyalty. No purchasing agent decides whether the company should buy greeting cards, or wheel housings, or insurance, or lighting or tubing or insulation. No factory floor engineer unilaterally decides he will change the parts used to assemble the product. The job of the purchasing agent, the factory floor engineer, is to implement a decision—to buy or change or whatever—made from above. In good companies, the "above" is that person(s) who is taking orders from the customer, the marketplace. The customer says, "I want a smaller-sized product." The marketing person knows what the "smaller-sized product" is worth. The marketing person knows that they can sell X more smaller products at Y price. X times Y equals the value of the smaller product. If your component, say a heat sink device, can help the customer make a television set smaller, then your heat sink is worth a percentage of X television sets times Y price. That percentage is the dollarized value of your heat sink.

Convince marketing of the dollarized value of your product, and marketing will convince engineering to give you the edge. And if you first call on marketing, you will be first in the product-selection process. If you first call on engineering, you are late to the product-selection process. If you first call on purchasing, you are last in the product-selection process.

Call on marketing. No one else does. Yet marketing makes the decisions by which customers buy products. Marketing makes Rainmakers money.

• XLII •

Don't Mail Proposals

*G*ood proposals, when mailed to the customer, have a winning percentage of 15 to 18 percent. Good proposals, when presented in person, have a winning percentage of 55 to 65 percent. Therefore, don't mail proposals. Present your proposal in person to the person(s) who can say "yes."

Good proposals must be able to sell without human help. But it is still a lot easier for a customer to reject a proposal that appears in the in-box than it is to say "no" to the person presenting the proposal.

Printed proposals can't ask for the order; people can ask for the order. People who ask for the order make more sales than people who don't ask for the order. People who present proposals and ask for the order win four times more sales than people who mail in proposals.

Geography, travel schedules, calendar events sometimes necessitate mailing the proposal. But if it is possible to present in person, and the proposal is mailed, that mailing is an act of selling cowardice. The seller fears rejection and goes MIA. The seller may not believe in the proposal, the product or service, or the price. Whatever the reason, a mailed proposal is oft a failed proposal.

Proposals presented in person have higher success rates because the presenter, the Rainmaker, believes in the recommendation. The Rainmaker believes in the fairness of the price and in the dollarized value of the customer's outcome. This belief in the product is obvious to the customer. The Rainmaker's confidence makes the customer confident. The Rainmaker will confidently ask the customer, "Based on your comments, this proposal meets your needs. Can we schedule the next step?" Then the Rainmaker waits for the customer to decide.

When the customer agrees to meet you to review your proposal, that is a buy signal. If the customer were disinclined to hire you or buy from you, he or she would duck such a meeting. The customer may negotiate, change course, add to the work scope, but the customer is ready to proceed.

People buy from people, not from pretty proposals. Don't abdicate your selling to the post office, to the pony express, or to any express mail.

time period. (You will have to choose probabilities based on your experience.) Multiply column two times column three. Put this number in column four, titled "Mean Expected Value," or MEV. The column gives the dollarized MEV—derived by multiplying the Probability of Close times the Potential Revenues.

SALES OF OPPORTUNITIES	POTENTIAL REVENUE	PROBABILITY OF CLOSE	MEV

• XLIII •

Use the MEV Sales Success Prioritization System

Here is how to prioritize your sales opportunities. Make a spreadsheet. Title column one "Sales Opportunities." Under this heading, list all your known target opportunities. Column two is titled "Potential Revenues." Potential revenue is the dollar revenue represented by the opportunity. (There are various ways to determine the potential sales revenue of an opportunity: e.g., units of product times selling price per unit, contract value, proposed project price.) Column three is titled "Probability of Close."

This column gives the probability percentage, say 40 percent, of closing the sale in the relevant sales time period. (You will read how to choose probability percentages in two minutes.) The fourth column is titled "Mean Expected Value," or MEV. This column gives numbers that are the result of multiplying the Probability of Close times the Potential Revenues.

This chart illustrates an opportunity spreadsheet.

SALES OPPORTUNITIES	POTENTIAL REVENUES	PROBABILITY OF CLOSE	MEV
New lawn, 53 Carey Avenue	$6,000	60%	$3,600
Landscape, 523 Coral Circle	$27,000	10%	$2,700
Stone wall, 15 Gilbert Hill	$11,000	20%	$2,200
Trim trees, 55 Shore Road	$2,000	90%	$1,800

There are two ways to prioritize the Sales Opportunities using this system. One way is to prioritize opportunities ranked by highest to lowest MEV. According to the chart, "New Lawn" has the highest MEV—$3,600—and therefore is a higher priority than the other three opportunities. The second priority route is to rank opportunities from highest Probability of Close to the lowest. According to the chart, "Trim trees," which has a close probability of 90 percent, would have the highest priority. Often it is best to pursue high Probability of Close opportunities first, and high MEV opportunities second. Note that "Landscape" is worth $27,000 in revenues if sold, but it has an MEV of $2,700. This means "Landscape," despite its high potential dollar value, is a lower priority.

The key to the MEV system is assigning Probabilities of Close. Each probability percentage must be event-based. This means that a probability is assigned if a specific sales event takes place. For example, assume there are six events that lead to a sale. Give each event a probability percentage based on experience or research or a good guess. Here is an example of events (which may differ for every industry) and assigned probabilities.

EVENT	PROBABILITY OF CLOSE
Salesperson schedules appointment	10%
Customer requests salesperson	40%
Customer agrees with needs analysis	60%
Customer agrees with dollarization	75%
Customer agrees to product test	90%
Customer gives purchase order	99%

It does not matter if the probability percentages are a perfect reflection of reality. What matters is that they are assigned according to specific events, and not "hunched" by the salesperson.

Update the MEV chart monthly, and adjust priorities accordingly. This system enables the Rainmaker to invest his or her time on those sales opportunities that are most likely to generate the most revenues. Prioritize and prosper.

• XLIV •

When You Get the Blues

*E*ven the best Rainmakers, the ones that stand on the top of the hill, and yell back at the thunder and lightning, and who will put their heads into the jaws of a pit bull to make the sale, sometimes get the . . . .

> *I'm just so sick of it,*
> *Tired of it,*
> *Don't want to do it,*
> *Can't hack it,*

Get me out of it,
I ain't selling no more,
Down and out blues.

Even the best, doing everything right, go zero for twenty, get mired in a slump, and hear the boos and whistles from the scorekeepers and the bookkeepers. Even the best drop the sure catch. Even the best hear the awful sound of a silent register.

So what do you do and don't do when you get the "I just want to pull the covers over my head" blues?

- Mentally blank out your slump. Go cold. Depersonalize. Poker-face your brain.
- Don't give in and get down.
- Don't second-guess yourself.
- Don't get mad at the walk-away customer.
- Don't get mad at people in your company.
- Don't say, write, or think a bad word about the customer who says "no."
- Get up an hour earlier, or leave work an hour early, and vigorously exercise for forty to sixty minutes.

- Objectively review recent lost sales. Do a sales autopsy. What went wrong? Lessons learned?
- Call a salesperson friend and trade tales of woe.
- Call every customer you lost at least six months ago and ask how everything is going.
- Dig deep into your internal, eternal fuel tank of optimism, competitiveness, energy, and positivism, and reload.

Remember you are good. Good things will happen. You are a Rainmaker. Make it rain.

EPILOGUE

Always be nice to everyone. It costs nothing. Being nice lowers your blood pressure. Being nice is a selling secret. Being nice evaporates any attack on you by a not-nice person. By being nice, maybe the customer will come to like you or like you more. Being nice will lead to more business.

MEET THE RAINMAKERS

Here are the Rainmakers who contributed their secrets to this book. For protection purposes the Rainmakers are not linked to their secrets or stories in the book. So, in alphabetical order, starting after "Anonymous," meet the Rainmakers.

Meet a Rainmaker

Thank you, Anonymous. Your company and colleagues know who you are. Your customers certainly know you. And now lots of new Rainmakers know how you ring the cash register.

Meet a Rainmaker

Like many Rainmakers, Russ Beemer was a Boy Scout. Boy Scouts learn to be prepared, to plan, to lead, and to work with others. Today he turns big problems into big sales. He prices products to value, not to cost, and does not discount. Russ is now national sales manager for a leading specialty seal company based in California.

Meet a Rainmaker

Brandon Bergstrom runs marathons. He runs be it rain or shine. He runs any distance for a client. As a financial adviser with Morgan Stanley, one of the world's most esteemed financial institutions, Brandon has grown his production over 30 percent year after year, every year. Starting with zero clients, zero contacts, and zero sales experience, he now manages over $100,000,000. Rainmakers run in the rain to make it rain. See Brandon run.

Meet a Rainmaker

Henrik Bruntse is an international Rainmaker. He is Danish, and based in Amsterdam. He can make deals in Danish, Dutch, English, German, Spanish, Swedish, some Norwegian, and a word or two in *autre lingua*. He is sales director, Northern Europe and the United Kingdom, for a specialty engineered parts company. *Cheers. Skal. Proost. Salud. A votre santé!*

Meet a Rainmaker

Michael Chen is a vice president and officer of GE Capital, and general manager of GE's aviation leasing and financing business in North America. GE has more than 1,300 aircraft worth $37 billion, and North America represents more than half the business. Michael was born in New York City and early on learned deal-making on the streets of that great city. The next time you see a plane, you see Michael.

Meet a Rainmaker

Jay Casbarro is a salesman for IKON, a Fortune 500 company that sells the best office equipment in the world. Here are Jay's selling stats. First year selling, Rookie of the Year. Second year, President's Club. Third year, promoted and named to President's Club and Million Dollar Club. Fourth year, promoted and named to President's Club. Fifth year, 150 percent over sales plan and President's Club. IKON has over 5,000 salespeople. Open the umbrella.

Meet a Rainmaker

Bill Davis began his career in the musical instrument business as a paratrooper with the fabled U.S. Army 82nd Airborne Division. As president of Kaman Music International, Bill parachuted into markets around the world selling woodwinds, brass instruments, and guitars. The sound of music is Rainmaker music.

Meet a Rainmaker

Steve Davis has been in commission sales since the start. He has won top sales awards throughout his career. For over a decade he has been number one in sales of retirement plans and assets gathered. Steve is national sales director for CitiStreet Corporate Markets Group, a joint venture between Citigroup and State Street Bank.

Meet a Rainmaker

Marco Dekker, born in Holland, was an internationally ranked badminton player, an individual sport that requires lightning reflexes and unwavering concentration . . . perfect training for a Rainmaker. As sales director, Europe, for an exceptional U.S. engineering company, Marco has tripled sales in three years. Badminton score: Marco 21, Competitors 0.

Meet a Rainmaker

After graduating from the College of the Holy Cross, Bill Farley built the Farley Company into a prominent regional commercial real estate company. He sold the company and is now a leading producer for CB Richard Ellis. In addition to making big deals, such as selling a $74,000,000 mall shopping center, Bill is a major benefactor to the poor. He has raised money and donated endless hours for the House of Bread, a charity that helps the down and out. Bill does well by doing good.

Meet a Rainmaker

Lou Gaudette sells lots of glue. Lou was a perennial member of the Sales Leadership Council, recognition for the top sellers. He is general sales manager for

Henkel Loctite's Automotive Aftermarket Division. Think glue, think Lou.

Meet a Rainmaker

Laurie Jelinek started at IBM as a sales representative trainee. She has held various sales and management positions in IBM, including vice president, Central Region, for small and medium businesses. Laurie has led many sales teams and has been recognized with several IBM sales awards in her career. She is now vice president of IBM's Global Emerging and Competitive Markets.

Meet a Rainmaker

Holly Lagsdin is an example of why the word "fan" comes from "fanatic." She is fanatical about the Boston Red Sox, and about baseball. She has closed many a deal eating stadium franks and diving for foul balls. In her career at General Electric she never missed a sales goal number! She is president of Stanley Specialty Tools.

Meet a Rainmaker

Ayn LaPlant's first job at the Beekley Corporation (Bristol, Conn.) was as sales coordinator. Several jobs later she is president and CEO. The Beekley Corporation is the world leader in innovating and selling marking products to the medical imaging and hotel industries. One factor in Beekley's perennial robust growth is that Ayn interviews every new associate. Beekley's opportunity-based culture makes it one of the best-work-environment small companies in the country.

Meet a Rainmaker

George Lucia has never lost a bottle rocket contest. His last Moosehead Ale bottle rocket is still flying, or so it is claimed. And he has rarely lost a customer. He earned his first, of countless, best-seller awards when he was a ten-year-old paperboy. (Ex-paperboys learn to deliver the goods.) George is senior vice president and general manager for the Bergquist Company, the world leader in thermal management materials, membrane switches, and touch screens.

Meet a Rainmaker

Like so many Rainmakers, Brad Mead started working when he was old enough to have a paper route. Whether selling papers or cutting tools, Brad is a natural. He has sold millions of cutting tools, which is why he is now vice president, Sales, for Valenite, a division of Sandvik AB, one of the world's first-class companies (Sandviken, Sweden). When he is not hunting for new sales, you will find Brad out in the fields upland bird game hunting with his two pointing dogs.

Meet a Rainmaker

Jody Moore is the fisherman's fisherman. He is a world-famous expert on saltwater fly-fishing, and has published over 120 magazine articles on that sporting art. In addition to showing Sylvester Stallone how to tie a fly, Jody has a real job. He is an owner of MSi Consulting and Ascent Solutions, two of Florida's leading accounting and computer employee placement firms. Jody is both firms' number-one business getter. Jody fishes where the big fish are and doesn't let the big ones get away.

Meet a Rainmaker

Ray Patrylak is a former Navy Top Gun "trouble-shooter." He was a member of the VF-31, the Navy's number-one fighter squadron, during the Vietnam War. His crews all came home. Wonder why Ray characterizes his selling strategy as the "Rules of Engagement"? Ray has been a President's Circle winner and top sales performer for such great companies as Rogers Corp and Saint-Gobain Corporation.

Meet a Rainmaker

T. Gary Rogers is chairman and CEO of Dreyer's Grand Ice Cream, Inc., the largest ice cream company in the United States. His career path to becoming a great Rainmaker included earning $1.00 a day as a paperboy and being an Eagle Scout. He was an Olympic class rower at the University of California at Berkeley. He was a Baker Scholar at the Harvard Business School. He started a restaurant company and went broke. Without any money he bought Dreyer's Grand Ice Cream. In two decades Dreyer's sales have grown from $6,000,000 to over $2,000,000,000. Only buy Dreyer's Grand Ice Cream.

Meet a Rainmaker

Jim Sittler's first job was cutting grass for neighbors. Jim sold the jobs, borrowed a lawn mower, cut the grass, collected the money, returned the lawn mower, then did it all again. Jim has been mowing 'em down ever since. Honorable Mention All-American soccer player. MBA. Comfortable in Mandarin and German.

Jim has never had a sales year worse than the previous year . . . not ever. He is vice president, Sales and Marketing, for Bal Seal Engineering in California.

Meet a Rainmaker

Francis "Chip" Traynor, Jr., worked on offshore oil rigs as a roughneck and a roustabout. One job was to build a board road through the Louisiana swamps. Each day the helicopters dropped the men and boards into the swamp. Sure-footedness was a must: Hundreds of swamp snakes would gather together in the brackish waters and all day long, in a big tangled ball, would slowly turn over and over. Chip got out of the swamps and became a stockbroker. He was named one of the top four brokers in the United States by the *New York Times*. He was the number-one broker at Shearson/American Express. He was elected chairman of the Chairman's Club. He built the Eden condo complex on Perdido Key, Florida. Chip is now managing director of Morgan Keegan Co. in Atlanta.

Meet a Rainmaker

At sixteen, Charles Vendetti started his career as a haberdasher (what a great name for an occupation!) brushing felt hats, returning shirt collars and cuffs to their proper place, and rehanging suits on racks. Charlie learned retail selling from the masters, including Joseph Stackpole, personal merchant and tailor to governors, senators, cardinals, archbishops, titans of industry. Charlie learned well and carried on the tradition of exemplary tailoring and service. From Maine to Miami, from Manhattan to Manhattan Beach, Charles Custom Clothiers, LLC (Avon, Conn.), travels to discriminating clients, providing custom and special-order men's clothing, shirts, and accessories. Rainmakers are the best-dressed people they will see that day.

Meet a Rainmaker

Mallory Walker is indeed a walker (a casual stroll is a fast five-mile trek in the Idaho mountains) and a bicycler and a white-water rafter and a Rainmaker. Mallory built Walker & Dunlop (Washington, D.C.) into a premier real estate finance firm specializing in asset management, and equity and mortgage financing for apartments, hotels, retail malls, mixed-use developments, and other commercial properties. His résumé, including thirteen years as a director of Fannie Mae (NYSE), is a virtual "what's what" in real estate. When Mallory is not doing deals, or walking, or fly-fishing in the mountain stream that runs through his backyard, he serves as a trustee of the Heinz Endowments in Pittsburgh.

Meet a Rainmaker

Penny Woodford sells houses and houses and houses. She is a member of Coldwell Banker's International President's Elite Club. She is perennially number one in every sales category in one of the most competitive markets in the country. She is a bank director and an expert in American Colonial antiques and historical homes, and owns and shows horses. She is one of the hardest-working real-estate agents in the country.

Meet a Rainmaker

Merrill Yavinsky was a scholarship student in college, and a scholar athlete: Dean's List and starting quarterback. He is a principal in Green Park Financial, one of the country's leading financiers of multi-family housing. Merrill is a big producer, a big Rainmaker. In thirty years Merrill has shepherded deals worth billions of dollars. Merrill has been scoring touchdowns all his life.

How to Become CEO

The Rules for Rising to the Top
of Any Organization

Jeffrey J. Fox

In recent years, the CEO's position within the typical high-profile company has been receiving more media attention than ever before. The job and paycheque of a CEO can quickly turn a relatively unknown top-level manager into a powerful international business leader with celebrity status. But how do those people get so lucky? What's their secret? Employees and recent graduates everywhere are asking, 'How can I get ahead?', 'How can I become CEO?'.

In *How to Become CEO*, consultant Jeffrey Fox has written an insightful handbook of traits to develop for anyone who wants to be CEO – or for anyone who just wants to get ahead in today's business world. Open it at any page and find a short, provocative piece of brutally honest advice written in a conversational tone. These are smart, no-nonsense business messages that are meant to be revisited in your rise to the top.

This book of hard-headed idealism will empower you to develop the qualities that are required of leaders: vision, persistence, integrity, and respect for superiors, subordinates, peers, and self.

If you want to climb the corporate ladder Fox's direct, pithy advice will help you to reach the top.

How to Become a Rainmaker
The Rules for Getting and Keeping
Customers and Clients

Jeffrey J. Fox

If identifying, attracting, getting and keeping customers are
your goals then this is the book you need. If you want to become invaluable to your organisation then find out *How to
Become a Rainmaker*.

Rainmakers are the people who bring money into their
organisation. They come in many guises including CEO,
owner, partner, sales representative, managing director or
fundraiser.

Rainmakers are not born. They are made. Jeffrey J. Fox
explains in his witty, succinct style how you too can be a rainmaker. His surprising, daring and totally practical wisdom
will help you to woo, pursue and finally win any customer;
and ultimately rise above the competition in any company.

How to Become a Rainmaker is packed full of wisdom
such as:

- Customers don't care about you
- Sell on Friday afternoons
- You are not at lunch to eat lunch

How to Become a Rainmaker is *the* recipe for how to sell,
for how to make rain, be it drizzle, deluge, sprinkle or storm!

Don't Send a CV

And Other Controversial Rules
to Help Land a Great Job

Jeffrey J. Fox

The workplace is now smarter and more competitive than ever. The real plum jobs are out there, but they're harder to get. Bestselling author and innovative thinker, Jeffrey J. Fox, comes to the rescue again with this no-nonsense collection of surprising and daring rules for landing the right job. Easy to read, inspiring and often counterintuitive, these concise ideas reflect the values of creative thinking that have made Fox one of the world's most emulated businessmen. He has had proven success with all of his rules including:

- CVs don't sell
- Don't ask for directions
- Make a big splash...not lots of little ripples
- Don't talk in an interview

Fox also has a jobseeker's glossary and a job-getting blueprint. His rules not only help you devise a winning strategy, but also show you how to prepare for and make the best impression in an interview. This wisdom-packed book will give you the edge on the competition and help prepare you for the challenges and rewards of landing not just a good job, but a great one.

How to Become a Great Boss
Winning Rules for Getting and Keeping the Best Employees

Jeffrey J. Fox

If you're a boss, hope to become one, or even if you have a second-rate boss, this is the book that could change your career – and your life.

The workplace is now smarter and more competitive than ever, so it pays for managers to be alert to the ways that good staff can be attracted and motivated. If you want surprising and useful advice on how to handle difficult situations – from having to sack a long-time employee to being a new boss with a demoralised staff – the stories, observations and advice contained in this book will point you in the right direction.

Renowned for his innovative approach to business, Jeffrey J. Fox has come up with this pithy and effective collection of rules and anecdotes to acquire great workers and achieve motivation in the workplace. His stories from bosses who have cared equally for employees' lives and the bottom line will inspire you to see that profit counts, but so do camaraderie, motivation and an exciting workplace.

How to Become a Marketing Superstar
Essential Rules of Business Success

Jeffrey J. Fox

In his previous bestselling business books, Jeffrey J. Fox has helped readers land great jobs and rise to the top of their professions. Now he turns his unconventional eye to marketing through brand building and innovation. Fox's advice is delivered in snappy, succinct chapters that zero in on his creative and often counterintuitive advice and features such unforgettable fundamentals as:

- Make a big splash, instead of a lot of little ripples
- Always have a pipeline to the CEO
- Own a market, not a mill
- The long and the short definitions of marketing

There are also provocative 'Instant Marketing Superstar' challenges throughout the book, offering the reader a chance to solve real business problems.

How to Become a Marketing Superstar is certain to find a place on the shelves of anyone who wants to increase sales in a competitive marketplace.

How to Make Big Money in Your Own Small Business

Unexpected Rules Every Small Business Owner
Needs to Know

Jeffrey J. Fox

A practical, original and inspiring guide for anyone wanting
to run a successful small business.

With only about half of small businesses still trading after
the first three years, setting up and surviving as an entrepreneur can be a tough game. Bestselling author Jeffrey Fox
has come up with a winning formula for small business owners to guarantee themselves commercial success and, what is
more, make big money in the process.

This book offers simple, practical and unique advice on
every aspect of running a small business, from how to get
start-up money to staying in profit. Fox also provides more
creative and quirky insights into how to be successful, such as
why you should:

- Not work from home
- Hire an ex-paperboy instead of a Harvard graduate
- Pick up paperclips but overspend on your customers

Whether you're already a small business owner or are simply
contemplating becoming one, this guide is essential reading.

Buy Vermilion Books

Order further Vermilion titles from your local bookshop, or
have them delivered direct to your door by Bookpost

Also available by Jeffrey J. Fox

☐ How to Become CEO	9780091826611	£8.99
☐ How to Become a Rainmaker	9780091876548	£8.99
☐ Don't Send a CV	9780091884277	£8.99
☐ How to Become a Great Boss	9780091887711	£8.99
☐ How to Become a Marketing Superstar	9780091891657	£8.99
☐ How to Make Big Money in Your Own Small Business	9780091900168	£8.99

FREE POST AND PACKING
Overseas customers allow £2.00 per paperback

ORDER:

By phone: 01624 677237

By post: Random House Books
c/o Bookpost
PO Box 29
Douglas
Isle of Man, IM99 1BQ

By fax: 01624 670923

By email: bookshop@enterprise.net

Cheques (payable to Bookpost) and credit cards accepted

Prices and availability subject to change without notice.
Allow 28 days for delivery.
When placing your order, please mention if you do not wish to receive
any additional information

www.randomhouse.co.uk